THE I CHING
for ROMANCE and FRIENDSHIP

THE I CHING
for ROMANCE and FRIENDSHIP

advice, insight and guidance
for all your personal relationships

ROSEMARY BURR

Eddison Books Ltd

In memory of my parents, Berenice and Reg.

British Library Cataloguing-in-Publication data available on request.

1 3 5 7 9 10 8 6 4 2

ISBN 978-1-8590-6464-1

Printed in China

CONTENTS

Introduction

This book is a modern version of the ancient Chinese Book of Changes (*I Ching*), which dates back thousands of years and is one of the most revered oracles in the world. Over the centuries it became a crucial part of traditional Chinese life and thought, and today still gives its users insight into the forces operating at a particular time. Its relevance and use have spread since the nineteenth century, its wisdom slowly filtering through to the West. I discovered the I Ching over forty years ago, and in my work as therapist and healer have turned increasingly to it when asked for specific practical advice, particularly on relationships.

In this version of the I Ching I've tried to reflect the oracle's inner spirit, removing any cultural veneer with no universal meaning while also keeping its precise quality. I hope I've stayed true to the universal nature of the principles expressed in the I Ching, as this is what makes it such a valuable tool of transformation and insight.

WHAT DOES THE FUTURE HOLD?

While there's an understandable desire to know what's going to happen, in terms of the I Ching this is the wrong question to ask. The I Ching is essentially pragmatic and (like many spiritual philosophies) stresses a need to be alive to the nuances of the current moment. It increases our awareness of the present and its potential for flowering into 'multiple futures', letting us maximize current opportunities and minimize possible pitfalls. It doesn't tell us what *will* happen, but shows us what *may* occur if we do nothing and if we can improve the outcome by acting in a certain way.

The I Ching's ability to get to the core of the matter is what makes it so invaluable. We often see our own thoughts, aspirations and fears reflected back to us rather than seeing the other person 'in the moment'. We act from habit, a unique model of the world we've built, usually made up of conflicting associations and beliefs. This book lets us discover the value of right action based on being true to oneself, aware of each person's own spiritual path and the need to act in harmony with our surroundings.

The oracle repeatedly stresses the importance of right timing and includes the idea of cycles. Events, like plants, grow from seeds to maturity, then finally die. We think life is stable, but we continually recreate our physical being and try to restore balance.

A TRANSFORMATION TOOL

By letting us view the core of our relationships this book helps us to enjoy a more fulfilling partnership. It's as if deep within us we have a precise, sensitive device that means we're drawn to certain people or situations and repulsed by others. We know there's something that makes one person our friend and another our foe, and this book gives that intangible element a pattern, image and name, which reflect the same qualities as the situation we are in. By producing a parallel image we can release our prior beliefs and emotions momentarily and look at the situation anew.

We have to nurture the potential for love and harmony in relationships, let it develop naturally and accept that it too will run its natural course. Each relationship is different because of its past experience – it will mature according to the thoughts we've planted. We must respect this growth process, honour the process of transformation and be alert to signs that the relationship is moving into new territory. Realigning ourselves with nature lets us improve our relationships with ourselves, others and the universe.

ABOUT THIS BOOK

This book gives simple, practical advice on any relationship question. All you do is throw the three coins provided six times to create a *hexagram*, a six-lined symbol representing a certain configuration of the I Ching's energies. There are sixty-four hexagrams in all, and the guidance associated with each is given on pages 14–141. Familiarize yourself first with the energies, or principles, the I Ching is based on, then follow the instructions on the next few pages, which explain how to take a reading.

Universal Principles

The I Ching is based on eight universal principles or natural laws: heaven, earth, water, thunder, mountain, wind, lake and flame. These principles, each represented by a three-line configuration known as a *trigram*, explain the often confusing and chaotic world which we call reality, and are at the heart of all situations we face. If we can tune into these principles, or elements of energy, through our own thoughts and transfer the energy signature into a hexagram, we can reach the core of the situation.

MODEL OF REALITY

The I Ching provides a model of reality that explains why change occurs and describes the underlying laws at work. It is based on the assumption of a division between spirit and matter; spirit gives birth to and includes within itself matter. We see reality as dualistic – male and female, yin and yang – but this is an illusion: the only difference between yang (represented by a solid line ———) and yin (a broken line — —) is the space in the middle of the line. Neither condition is stable, but constantly changing, which you'll see when you throw the coins to form a 'moving' line (*see page 11*).

UNIVERSAL HOLISM

The modern Western mind can find it hard to grasp the symbolism of the eight universal principles. Basically, heaven is the all-encompassing energy pouring forth its qualities on to the earth. These seven qualities each vibrate at their own level and have a different impact on the matter they come into contact with – one enlivens, one pacifies, one harmonizes, and so on. Similarly, we can view eight 'building bricks' of the I Ching – the eight trigrams (or energy packages) that interact with and stimulate matter.

Remember that we are just seeing a *part* of the whole. Life isn't black and white – we all have the potential to widen our vision, and this book will show you how to do just that.

THE EIGHT ENERGIES

The energies combine in pairs to form sixty-four hexagrams, but what do the eight energies represent?

Heaven This represents 'God', the 'Great Spirit' – the 'universal energy'. In terms of the oracle it also represents someone who channels this energy, God's messenger, a prophet, sage, pope or even a king. Heaven inspires and motivates us, and moves us to higher thoughts and feelings.

Earth Earth stabilizes us, provides a resting place – a place we can sow our seeds away from the harsh reality around us. We can nurture them until the time is right for the seedlings to emerge and flower. Earth helps to break down old patterns and thoughts, to transform negative into positive; garbage becomes manure.

Water Over time, water wears down rock. If you continue to be true to yourself then you can create change too. Just as water changes its form, so we can alter our appearance, but to be successful we must steer a life-path using our souls as guidance. Go within and find your own truth. Thus you stay true to yourself and events are transformed by your persistent actions.

Thunder Thunder creates a loud bang, which wakes people up from their slumber. The action of thunder is arousal – it indicates a situation that is overheated and has excess energy that needs to be channelled in a different form. Just as the air is clear after the thunder, so a good row brings conflicts into the open and provides the chance for resolution.

Mountain Mountains are large, still areas of energy, both obstacles and opportunities. They symbolize meditation and the raising of consciousness on the one hand, and outdated beliefs that have become obstacles on the other.

Wind Wind moves things from one place to another – it is a messenger, symbolizing communication, the spreading of ideas. But ideas alone don't create change – the catalyst for transformation is the person with the idea. Wind helps to create conditions where change may happen, but it can't stabilize or make these changes on earth.

Lake Lake is a receptacle on the earth for water (which represents our soul potential, activated through the heart). If we act according to our heart's desire, we feel happy and joyful; so lake's actions give us a cup overflowing with heart energy, bringing joy into our lives.

Flame Fire lights up our lives, letting us see at night and creating light out of darkness, but to make fire you need a spark and material to ignite. Flame's energy is social – to shine brightly, you must share your heart with others. Only then will your passion be turned into a healing and transforming flame.

Consulting the Oracle

This book is easy to use and it can help you obtain specific advice on what to do to make the most of your relationships. Here's how to consult the oracle:

1. Get a journal. This will become your sacred space to create a record of your readings.

2. Phrase your question. You need to make sure it's specific and time-related. For instance, don't ask 'Will I ever marry?', but rather 'Will this relationship with Oliver, say, lead to a proposal of marriage in the next year?' The clearer the question, the more helpful the advice. The I Ching is very practical and you'll gain maximum benefit from it if you ask straightforward, down-to-earth questions. Write down your question with the date and time.

3. Throw the coins. In order to get an answer to your question you need to create a hexagram – this is a symbol made of six lines. Each line is created by throwing all three coins together, once, and seeing whether the coins fall head-side (the side with four characters) or tail-side (the side with two characters) facing up.

THROWING THE COINS

For each throw, place the three coins in the palm of your left hand (your intuitive side) and put your right palm over the left, close your eyes, let any stressful thoughts fade away, imagine yourself in a bubble of clear sparkling light and mentally ask your question. Then throw the trio of coins six times. Each time the coins land you need to note which side is uppermost and make sure you record the throws in the correct order. You build from the bottom upwards, so the first throw forms the bottom line, the second throw the line above that, and so on. The box below shows you how to transcribe your result into a line in the hexagram, and the traditional way of recording each of the four possible outcomes.

Recording your throws	
IF YOU THROW	DRAW THIS LINE
3 tails	—x—
2 tails, 1 head	— —
2 heads, 1 tail	———
3 heads	—o—

If you happen to throw either three heads or three tails, this indicates that a change is about to occur in the situation. In order to highlight that change, either an 'x' or an 'o' is added to the line. This is referred to as a 'moving' line.

EXAMPLE

The first thing you need to do is throw the coins and record your results (*see box above*). Then you can create your hexagram. Remember that you must start at the bottom (*see right*).

1st throw	3 heads	6th throw — —
2nd throw	2 heads, 1 tail	5th throw ———
3rd throw	2 heads, 1 tail	4th throw —x—
4th throw	3 tails	3rd throw ———
5th throw	2 heads, 1 tail	2nd throw ———
6th throw	2 tails, 1 head	1st throw —o—

This is your first hexagram, which gives you the answer to your initial question. However, you can see that you have generated two moving lines (on the first throw and the fourth throw), which means that the situation you are asking about is shortly going to change. But, you may ask, how exactly is it going to change? The answer to this more specific question is revealed by constructing a second hexagram.

MOVING LINES

So what do you do if you throw a moving line? You retain the first hexagram but each moving line changes into its opposite. Thus: —x— becomes ———, and —o— becomes — —. This gives you your second hexagram. Look at the example shown below to see how this works in practice.

First hexagram
Second hexagram

Remember: don't alter the position of any of the lines, and only change moving lines.

FINDING YOUR READING

Once you've created your hexagrams, you can unlock the I Ching's wisdom. Check the table on page 144 to find the right page for your hexagram. Each hexagram gives advice on the overall situation, plus specific guidance to help you answer questions on new romance, existing partnerships and friendships. You'll also find timely tips on how to avoid pitfalls (*see key to symbols below*).

ⓞ EXISTING PARTNERSHIPS	ⓞ NEW ROMANCE	ⓝ FRIENDSHIP	⊗ PITFALLS

If your hexagram has moving lines, the guidance given for individual moving lines will give you extra insight. If you've created a second hexagram, read your hexagram's general commentary and the tips on avoiding problems to see how the situation will alter.

GETTING THE BEST FROM THE ORACLE

First, set some time aside to focus. Write down any associations, images or feelings that come to mind, then carefully formulate your question and jot this down as well. Ideally set aside half an hour to consult the oracle. Note down the hexagram and key words from the text and put aside any preconceptions when reading the reply. How do you feel? What do you want to pursue? The record sheet on page 142 will help you to note your initial consultations accurately. In most cases the response will be an obvious answer to your question, but if it isn't, take time to mull it over. If you really can't see any relevance, try again later.

A WORD OF CAUTION

This I Ching helps you to act wisely, based on an understanding of your own circumstances. It can help to create a path of joy and beauty, and encourages you to tune in directly to the situation's energies. This book helps you to detach from feelings of love, anger or jealousy (which can stop us receiving clear, helpful messages), reveals the truth faced in any situation, and helps to bring harmony to your own life and those of your loved ones.

A SAMPLE CONSULTATION

Question: Will Oliver propose this year?

Emily has been going out with Oliver for three years and she is getting fed up with his lack of commitment. She wants to know if he's finally going to propose to her this year. Her patience is running out and she's started to imagine all sorts of increasingly bizarre reasons why Oliver is stalling.

THROWING THE COINS

Emily concentrates on her question and throws the three coins six times. Her throws are shown to the right. This gives her her first hexagram (*see below right*). Remember that the first throw constitutes the bottom line, and so on.

Emily is pleased to see two moving lines, as she knows this means the deadlock is about to be resolved. She creates her second hexagram by transforming the moving lines into their opposite – that is, by changing ━x━ into ━━━ .

1st throw	2 heads, 1 tail
2nd throw	2 heads, 1 tail
3rd throw	2 heads, 1 tail
4th throw	3 tails
5th throw	2 heads, 1 tail
6th throw	3 tails

◀ *First hexagram*

Second hexagram ▶

INTERPRETING THE RESULTS

What does this mean for Emily's future with Oliver? The first hexagram is number 5, Pause for Thought; the second hexagram is number 1, Promise of Passion. Emily starts by reading the general commentary for hexagram 5, which tells her that the time is not yet right to force the issue. Then she checks the symbol for existing partnerships – the accompanying text tells her to enjoy herself rather than worrying about the future. Emily also checks the pitfalls. She is pleased to see that she must remain confident about the prospect of future happiness.

Emily's moving lines came on the fourth and sixth throws, so she checks these readings. They warn her that there are difficulties below the surface – something stressful may happen, but a new event will change things for the better. Armed with this information Emily turns to her second hexagram, Promise of Passion, which tells her that the best way to respond to the events highlighted by the first part of the reading is to take the initiative. Emily now knows she has to be patient, brace herself for bad news, then take appropriate action.

OUTCOME

Emily discovered that Oliver was still married to Sophie, whom he had not seen in five years. (Emily found out because Oliver's best friend told her that Oliver would never marry her as he hadn't yet divorced his first wife.) Emily decided to confront Oliver and tell him she knew about Sophie. She told him she loved him very much and wanted to marry him, and asked him to divorce Sophie. Oliver filed for divorce and proposed to Emily when he was a free man. Emily's patience and positive attitude paid off and she received her desired proposal.

1 PROMISE OF PASSION

Heaven
Heaven

The secret of maximizing the energy in this situation is correct action. Seize the initiative and go for what you know in your heart is the right solution. If you persist and remain true to yourself, you'll find success beyond your wildest dreams.

This is your chance to create a deep spiritual bond with your loved one. It's a time to look beyond the superficialities of the material world and see what impact the two of you are having on the world at large.

If you've just met someone, this could be the start of a true romance. Are you willing to risk opening your heart and sharing your true feelings? Now is the time to let go of power games and simply be yourself.

Your friendship can deepen considerably now. Together you have the strength and confidence to create something new, launch a revolutionary project or simply break down a few outdated social barriers.

Don't become too cocky, overbearing or tactless. Seize the moment, but don't believe you are invincible. Remember to share your good fortune with others and use your energy in a constructive way to create something of lasting value.

MOVING LINES

 Wait a short while before you take action. Something has yet to be revealed or someone else will appear on the scene.

 You may have just met the right person or have an inkling of the best course of action. Pursue these matters further.

 If you remain true to yourself, all will be well. Do not let popularity or playing the field obscure your heart's desire.

 You have a choice here: either to deepen the relationship or go your own way. Whichever path you choose, you can gain knowledge, wisdom and growth.

 Develop the relationship to its full potential, as there is great joy and mutual support available for you.

 Danger! Either you or your partner wrongly believe that you are invincible.

Extremely lucky and significant. Heaven is smiling on the pair of you.

○ EXISTING PARTNERSHIPS   ○ NEW ROMANCE   ○ FRIENDSHIP   ⊗ PITFALLS

2 OPEN TO IDEAS

Earth
Earth

It's a time to provide support for your loved ones. They need to be cherished, nurtured and encouraged to be themselves. Learn the art of listening without speaking.

How nurturing is your partnership? Ask yourself if you provide emotional, financial and spiritual support for each other. If not, how about setting some mutual goals and devising some strategies to achieve them?

Don't push your attentions on a new partner. Sit back, wait and listen instead. What sort of relationship is on the cards? Discover more before you take any action.

Check the status of your friendship. Who's been making the running, arranging the outings and paying the bills? Remember that unbalanced friendships do not last long.

With this energy it's very easy to become a yes-person or a couch potato. Instead, imagine how you'd like your life to be in the future. Think of lines of light linking you to these future events and drawing them to you.

MOVING LINES

There are some small tell-tale signs that all is not well in this relationship. However, it's still early enough to do something about this if you feel you want to.

This partnership will provide each of you with exactly what you need right now. There's no need for any conscious interference by either party.

There's the possibility of long-term gain from this partnership. However, it may mean that one or both of you will need to put some immediate short-term goals on hold.

Don't try to push the relationship at this time. You may need to step back for a little while or keep quiet on a key matter. Discretion is the watchword here.

Your partner's heart is true. Don't be misled by appearances, as their actions will speak volumes about their love for you.

Watch out! There is conflict in the air – bruising emotional exchanges and even possible temper tantrums.

This is a union made in heaven. You probably feel as if you are soul mates and have known each other all your lives.

© EXISTING PARTNERSHIPS   ② NEW ROMANCE   ⑩ FRIENDSHIP   ⊗ PITFALLS

3 A TRICKY START

Water
Thunder

This is a time of upheaval, of new beginnings, when you need to stay true to yourself. In order to make sense of what you are experiencing, you could consider talking it over with friends, perhaps even a counsellor.

Your partnership is entering a new phase, and rules you've lived by are now changing. Don't keep your doubts to yourself: talk them over with your partner. If you can't agree, then try some form of joint counselling.

You've chosen a challenging relationship with potential, but it's going to be rather fragile to start with. It can go the distance if both of you are honest and have integrity.

This suggests an unlikely friendship, forged by a mutual desire to change some aspect of yourselves. Don't let old habits, social etiquette or family squabbles get in the way.

Worthwhile relationships can take time to bloom, so don't give up. Be prepared to discover some unpleasant home truths along the way, though.

MOVING LINES

You are not in a position to handle this situation on your own.
Time and outside assistance will heal this relationship.

There are difficulties in your current relationship. The offer of
help from another person, or even an alternative partnership,
is tempting – but it is to be avoided.

This relationship has all sorts of problems. You should
consider looking somewhere else if you want to find
true happiness.

Help is needed if this relationship is to work. It's up to you to
sort things out, as your partner does not seem to realize the
urgency of the situation.

There's a lack of trust in this partnership. In order to win
your partner over, you must prove yourself to be reliable,
truthful and loving over time.

Sometimes there are just too many obstacles in the way of a
fruitful partnership. Instead, as here, it would be best simply
to cut your losses and leave.

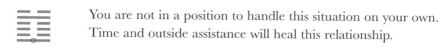

◐ EXISTING PARTNERSHIPS   ⊘ NEW ROMANCE   ◍ FRIENDSHIP   ⊗ PITFALLS

4 TESTING TIME

Mountain
Water

Something stands in the way of what you hope to achieve. You need to ask yourself exactly why you're attracted to this relationship and whether you truly believe that it is right. If it is, you will need to prove yourself to the other person by sheer persistence, integrity and consistency. Only you know whether this is a whim or true love.

 Are you stopping your partner achieving something, or are they blocking you? Either way, there's a genuine fear that if you follow your heart's desire you'll lose the other person. Talk things through together.

 If you've just met, listen carefully. Pause, reflect and – before you make any move to further this relationship – be certain of your motives.

 A clever person learns from their own mistakes; a wise one, from other people's. What can your friends teach you now? And how can you help them see what's blocking their path?

Self-deceit is likely to play a part here. Who are you kidding? Remember: you'll be the one carrying the can here, both emotionally and spiritually.

MOVING LINES

 You may be tempted to play the field, but you will soon discover that this doesn't bring lasting happiness.

 If you are faced with a partner with weaknesses they can't resolve, you can help them by creating inner strength.

 Don't try to compensate for your own shortcomings by finding a partner you think has the qualities you seek. Focus instead on nurturing these qualities in yourself.

 Is this a relationship or a fantasy? You need to do a reality check. Ask the other person what they feel, rather than taking advantage of their affection.

 If you approach this relationship with an open heart and a willingness to explore new ways of communicating with people, you will benefit immensely.

 No one should have to put up with a painful relationship. It's time to stand up for yourself and, if necessary, get some outside assistance. That way you can stop the situation occurring again.

5 PAUSE FOR THOUGHT

Water
Heaven

This is a time of inner reflection and healing. Trust yourself and your connection to the universe. You need to develop inner strength, faith and the ability to recognize intuitively when the time is right to act. Circumstances will improve shortly and you will be glad you waited.

 Enjoy this partnership. Take time to listen to each other, be playful and celebrate your relationship.

 If you have just met someone, don't expect romance to flourish straight away. The long-term outlook is excellent, so relax and treat yourself to your favourite night out.

 Friendship, like fine wine, can take time to mature. Don't push things yet.

 Stay true to your original wish, but don't focus on how it might be achieved. Fate is on your side, so enjoy the anticipation of future happiness.

MOVING LINES

   Don't let fear or worry about not being in a relationship lead you to commit prematurely to something that's not right for you.

   Don't get dragged into arguments, criticize other people or publicize their shortcomings. Just wait and see what develops.

   Your emotions are muddling your responses and you have switched to automatic pilot based on outdated beliefs. Realize that you are entering a difficult situation. When in doubt, don't act.

   You're in a tricky situation, which could be worsened by hasty action. Do nothing to aggravate the situation further.

   Learn to live in the moment and enjoy the relationship for what it offers today. Greater emotional nourishment will be forthcoming if you're patient and don't provoke any conflict.

   Just when you think the relationship has reached its lowest ebb, a stroke of luck or outside event radically alters your perspective. Reassess the situation and see whether this new element will give you what you need for emotional fulfilment.

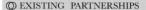

6 CLASH OF PASSION

Heaven
Water

Communication is the key to resolving conflict. In your current situation, there is a temptation to ignore the underlying differences and move ahead regardless. It is advisable to clarify and resolve all the details of your relationship before pressing for greater commitment.

 Are you taking each other for granted? Try setting aside an hour a week for each of you to air your grievances and devise a strategy to resolve any difficulties.

 This is a testing time for a new relationship. Some fundamental issues need to be resolved before the partnership can flourish.

 What is the purpose of this friendship? Unless you are prepared to thrash out a mutually acceptable solution, conflicting values may stop it going any further.

 Don't ignore differences and try to override your partner. You may need outside help from a counsellor to resolve your dilemma successfully.

MOVING LINES

Try to avoid blowing up small issues into major conflicts. If you can stay centred, this emotional storm will pass quickly. Try to focus on joint long-term goals rather than short-term obstacles.

This is a battle you are unlikely to win. Do not waste your emotional energy on such a draining situation. Be brave, admit defeat and start to consider your options. Remember that when one door shuts, another opens.

Stick to what you believe to be right and don't let anyone seduce you into changing your mind or what you plan to do. You will meet with disappointment and frustration if you alter your plans.

You feel unsettled and would like to change the current situation. However, if you avoid confrontation, circumstances will eventually improve. For the moment, spend some quality time on yourself.

If you know you are in the right, then now is the time to enlist the assistance of an impartial adviser. Your goal is achievable in the near future. However, you need some independent guidance to make the process less painful.

You may win this battle, but then you will lose the war. Which is more important: your ego or the relationship? Take stock of your priorities and act accordingly.

Ⓞ EXISTING PARTNERSHIPS   ⦷ NEW ROMANCE   ⦿ FRIENDSHIP   ⊗ PITFALLS

7 POWER PLAY

Earth
Water

One of the keys to a successful relationship is to have a set of clearly defined mutually acceptable goals. Once you have agreed these goals you can develop strategies for achieving them. This is a time to get strategic and ensure you are working in harmony to develop the resources you need to achieve your goals together.

 Take time to agree a relationship plan for your partnership. Spell out your desires, wishes and needs. Then, fine-tune your goals in ways that are clear and achievable.

 Check the other person's game plan. Are you both looking for the same level of passion and commitment?

 Discuss how you wish to spend your time together. Reassess old patterns in the light of your current needs.

 Does one person in this relationship have a hidden agenda? Make sure you both communicate clearly what it is you have to gain from this relationship – this will avoid any future disappointment.

MOVING LINES

If you can't agree on issues such as commitment, finance and family, then the outcome is poor. Cut your losses now before you become more involved emotionally.

Each of you has unique gifts and talents to contribute to this relationship. If you give freely of your time and energy, success is assured. Stick with it.

Make sure each of you knows exactly what you are expected to contribute. If you let outsiders interfere, problems will arise. Talk to each other more often and try to take a more active interest in each other's passions.

It is time to reassess your goals and release unrealistic expectations that may be weighing heavily on one or both of you. Seek outside help from a counsellor if necessary, as they can help you to identify the key areas requiring change.

You may need to check your finances, home security and ensure that anyone giving you advice is indeed impartial. Don't take people at face value. Read the small print before you sign any agreements.

Your initial goals are achieved. Make sure that each of you is rewarded for the time and effort invested. Do not fritter away your success mindlessly, but continue to build your relationship.

◎ EXISTING PARTNERSHIPS   ② NEW ROMANCE   ⑩ FRIENDSHIP   ⊗ PITFALLS

8 MAGNETIC ATTRACTION

Water
Earth

There is a strong magnetic attraction here, but it is important to develop the relationship at a steady and even pace. The time to strengthen and enhance this bond is right now. Check whether the other person is available and willing to go for a lasting commitment, if that is what you seek.

There is an opportunity to create a wonderful long-term relationship which is mutually satisfying and fulfilling. Make sure you explore all your options.

This could well be the real thing. Don't hesitate – give yourself plenty of time to explore the potential of this partnership. If you are ready, go for commitment.

Friendships need nurturing. This one is well worth investing further time and extra energy in – now. Do not delay.

Persistence, integrity and commitment are all vitally important. Make sure your partner is prepared for the long haul; otherwise you face emotional burn-out.

MOVING LINES

 You are on to a winner here. There is a sincere desire by your partner to make the relationship work. Spend more time together and do not allow small difficulties to escalate into major problems.

 Don't try to alter your behaviour, looks or clothes to capture the other person's heart. They will value you for your true self. Make sure that you express your ideas clearly, and don't get defensive if your partner doesn't agree with your point of view.

 Although there is an initial attraction, sadly there's no stable foundation to this relationship. Keep it light-hearted and remain open to other possibilities. Try to widen your circle of friends and explore other partnerships.

 There's a strong mutual bond here. Don't be tempted to take it for granted. Avoid exploring other relationships that could jeopardize this one. Try to communicate more openly and honestly with your partner.

 Do not put pressure on your partner to commit. If the relationship is to flourish, then it will do so in an atmosphere of openness and flexibility. Patience is crucial now; otherwise you will scare them away.

 Things got off on the wrong footing and the relationship can never grow in this form. Start looking further afield for a new relationship. Focus on the qualities you are seeking from a partner rather than their outward appearance.

① EXISTING PARTNERSHIPS ② NEW ROMANCE ③ FRIENDSHIP ⊗ PITFALLS

INITIAL DALLIANCE

Wind
Heaven

This is a time to have fun and explore who you are. Enjoy this relationship for what it is right now, without worrying or planning the future. Learn simply to be in the moment and thankful for everything you have.

If you are frustrated about a lack of progress on a particular issue, hold your fire. This is not the time to make a stand or force a confrontation.

Take things easy. Try to avoid playing any mind games that would pressurize the other person into taking a firm stance on a controversial issue.

This is a wonderful opportunity to enjoy a light-hearted friendship. Don't get involved in analysing the other person's behaviour or words.

Don't push to deepen this relationship at this time. Wait and see how things develop. There are certain factors about this person which you need to discover and understand before you can make an informed decision.

MOVING LINES

 Don't be afraid to withdraw an ultimatum. You will find the situation resolves itself naturally and automatically – as long as you retreat gracefully and don't force your partner into a humiliating position.

 If you are considering issuing some form of ultimatum or deadline, keep quiet for the moment. Seek the advice of some like-minded friends on how best to tackle the situation.

 The issue you are considering is not as straightforward as you imagine. If you try to press for a solution, you will receive a strong rebuff. Take time to discover the full facts and explore alternative ways of solving the difficulty.

 If you are concerned about the other person's wellbeing, then you will be able to secure the changes you seek by remaining sincere and consistent. Patience, persistence and compassion are your recipe for success.

 The key to success here is staying faithful to the other person in word and deed. Try to avoid gossip or loose talk that could be misinterpreted. Do not be tempted to confide in friends and family. Keep your own counsel for the present.

 You may have achieved your goal by gently and persistently wearing down the opposition. However, now is not the time to press home your advantage. Be generous and caring in your current dealings with your partner.

10 PASSION PLAY

Heaven
Lake

Would you grab a tiger by its tail and pull hard? Not unless your survival instincts were in bad shape. This is not the time to act: either the issue can't be resolved right now or the person involved has too much emotion invested in continuing the status quo.

You can ride this storm by not getting drawn into arguments about the progress of your relationship or controversies about third parties.

Take your time to discover your partner's strengths and weaknesses. Avoid verbal confrontations and set clear guidelines on how you expect to be treated.

This is likely to be a shaky patch. One or other of you is going through an intense reaction to a certain situation and will need kindness and understanding.

If in doubt, take time out from this relationship. Control your emotions and don't get embroiled in destructive arguments. Your partner may need to seek counselling to improve their communication skills.

MOVING LINES

 If you stick to your principles and develop the relationship slowly, you will make the most of this partnership. Enjoy the moment and try not to second-guess your partner's response to situations.

 Do not place demands on the other person's time or energy. If the relationship is to thrive they will make the running. Be patient in the short term and try not to become clingy or demanding.

 Either you do not have the full facts or your emotions are clouding your judgement. Try to bide your time if you wish to avoid disappointment. A friend or family member may be able to throw further light on the situation.

 You are faced with a genuine problem, but you do not have sufficient emotional and social resources to resolve it successfully. Seek help from friends or family. Try to remember situations in the past where you have overcome similar obstacles.

 You know your situation is fraught with difficulties, but you are determined to persist with a particular course of action. Be strong and trust your instincts.

 If you have acted throughout with honesty and integrity you will enjoy the rewards of a satisfying and fulfilling relationship. Any double-dealing will backfire badly on you.

Ⓒ EXISTING PARTNERSHIPS   ⊘ NEW ROMANCE   ⓪ FRIENDSHIP   ⊗ PITFALLS

11 EMOTIONAL HARMONY

Earth
Heaven

Awonderful time to enjoy and explore any relationship you find yourself in – when your every impulse and desire seems to be in tune with that of the other person. You can create a new level of intimacy and also provide each other with the emotional support needed to achieve your material goals.

 Celebrate your togetherness in new ways. Explore all the possibilities in this relationship. Let your dreams come true.

 A magical start to your relationship. You will have the opportunity to grow and learn while enjoying passion and love.

 True friendship can blossom and grow now. There is a deep intuitive understanding and willingness to support each other in whatever path you choose.

 Make the most of this phase while it exists. Do not expect this honeymoon period to last for ever. Learn to savour the moment and develop your passion for life.

MOVING LINES

 Use this period of emotional stability as a launch pad to improve all your relationships, particularly those with family members that may have been under strain recently. You can afford to extend the hand of friendship to those people who in the past appeared distant and cool.

 Make an effort to share your good feeling with friends and family. If they need support and assistance, open your heart to them. This is a time to develop your social skills and show how caring you can be to those in genuine need.

 Keep working at your relationship. Be grateful for this wonderful period, but realize that you still need to invest time and energy in this partnership to maintain its momentum. The results will be worthwhile and will add vitality to the partnership.

 You may find yourself in the role of teacher. Share your experiences freely with others and use their responses to help you increase your understanding of relationships.

 This is a time of great happiness, nurturing and support. Look beyond people's outer circumstances and connect to their potential. You have a wonderful opportunity for contentment, calmness and creativity.

 This period of harmony is coming to its natural conclusion. If you try to extend it, you will fail. Be thankful that you have been blessed with the gift of such a wonderful time of sharing.

Ⓞ EXISTING PARTNERSHIPS   ⵔ NEW ROMANCE   ⵖ FRIENDSHIP   ⊗ PITFALLS

12 TEMPTATION

Heaven
Earth

Contrary to what appears on the surface, this is not a time to be lured into a new relationship or tempted by an offer of friendship. It would be far better to channel your energy and support in other directions.

 The key issue here is trust. Follow your intuition – if you feel concerned by some undercurrent, or suspect that all is not what it seems, follow your instinct.

 This is a push–pull situation. Something about this relationship is hooking you in, but your inner voice is advising caution. Listen to your feelings.

 An offer of assistance or an introduction to another person is not what it seems. When in doubt, do not confide in others.

 This is definitely a time to keep your thoughts and ideas to yourself. However attractive other people's ideas or offers appear on the surface, they are not right for you and could lead to both practical and emotional problems.

MOVING LINES

 It is best to withdraw gracefully from this situation. You will find help and assistance from an unexpected source. An older person may provide the clue you need to make sense of this particular emotional puzzle.

 Although the situation appears unfavourable, by sticking to your ideals and refusing to be lured into dangerous emotional waters you gain contentment. Keep your own counsel on this matter and do not listen to gossip.

 The person who is tempting you with false promises is beginning to have a change of heart. The situation is improving gradually and you will be glad you didn't get hooked into an untenable situation.

 You're beginning to think about what changes you would like to implement in the relationship. Follow your heart and you will find someone to share your vision.

 Now that you have avoided compromising your principles, the way ahead is clear. However, don't throw caution to the wind. Take each decision carefully and calmly and avoid making hasty sweeping conclusions.

The right offer comes along to end this period of temptation. You can see clearly the value of this new approach. It brings fulfilment and peace. Grab it eagerly.

◎ EXISTING PARTNERSHIPS   ⊘ NEW ROMANCE   ⍟ FRIENDSHIP   ⊗ PITFALLS

13 SOUL POTENTIAL

Heaven
Flame

This is a time to cherish a deep soul connection with another. You can help the other person to realize their true potential and star quality. Together you can create a mutually fulfilling relationship, which can be the foundation for your success in the world. However, you need to be totally honest with yourself and the other person about any existing obstacles to your partnership.

A deep soul union is possible at this time. Combine physical passion with emotional support and spiritual nourishment.

Although your relationship is new, it will feel familiar in an exciting way. It is as if you have known this person all your life.

You can support each other in wonderful ways at this time. You know instinctively what the other person needs in order to become more successful and fulfilled.

Avoid losing touch with reality and slipping into a dream world. Stay grounded and take care of your material responsibilities. Make sure the other person is being honest and open, and check that they are not involved with someone else.

MOVING LINES

It is very important to be open and honest. Listen to what the other person has to say. Do not assume that because you have such strong feelings you can ignore practical obstacles to your relationship.

Do not give up on friends and family. Although this relationship is passionate, you need to maintain emotional equilibrium and mental clarity. If you need time to yourself, take it without feeling guilty.

The situation is fraught with problems. One or both of you are carrying emotional baggage from the past, and this is obstructing your partnership.

Although there are barriers to this relationship, each party is prepared to address the problems. Success is in sight if you can each act with honesty, fidelity and integrity.

Despite a host of problems, you remain true to your heart's desire. Together you meet and conquer every obstacle in your path. Success is assured in time.

Complete union of mind, body and soul is not possible for mere human beings. However, you can cherish the special closeness you have in this relationship – it is the stuff of wonderful memories.

14 ECSTASY

Flame
Heaven

This is a wonderful opportunity for you to open your heart and discover a new sense of passion – a time to share your emotional fulfilment with others around you. You can help them to overcome their past emotional disappointments by offering them love and support.

 The obstacles to intimacy that you have each carefully constructed in order to prevent any more pain can now be dismantled. Your love life can become more exciting and communication improves dramatically.

 This is a time to open your heart and blow away any barriers which may have prevented you getting the love and commitment you needed in the past.

 Friendship can now grow and flourish. There is a greater sense of harmony and synchronicity.

 It is important to widen your circle of friends and open your heart in as many new ways as possible. Do not bury yourself in one relationship or become addicted to one person's presence.

MOVING LINES

 There are problems to be faced and it would be helpful to discuss potential issues of contention openly and calmly. Make more time for communication.

 You have the support of family and friends. Be sure to call on their help whenever you need someone to help you resolve your problems. Don't be too proud to ask for support.

 Don't take advantage of the one you say you love. The more open and loving you become, the more support and care you will receive. Remember: what you sow, you reap.

 You may have to contend with jealousy or a third party trying to interfere in your relationship. Don't get dragged into arguments about outsiders. Stay true to your own values and feelings.

 In some way, you are seen as a role model. Your relationship is closely scrutinized by others. Remain true to yourself at all times. If you compromise your principles, there will be a domino effect of pain and trauma.

 This is a truly magical time, when your relationships can flourish and you can connect easily and intensely with people from all walks of life. Celebrate and count your blessings now.

◐ EXISTING PARTNERSHIPS   ⊘ NEW ROMANCE   ⊗ FRIENDSHIP   ⊗ PITFALLS

15 RESTORING BALANCE

Earth
Mountain

There is a need to restore balance and harmony in your relationship. Check every aspect of your partnership. If your sex life is flagging, be more inventive. If communication is at a standstill, create a time when you can talk. Make sure you are nurturing your whole self. Take care of your physical health, emotional wellbeing and spiritual needs.

Have you slipped into unconscious patterns of behaviour that are debilitating? Make more time for each other. Try to balance the need to take care of family, friends and finances with the need to nurture each other.

If the attraction is purely sexual, get to know the other person. Learn to share your thoughts, feelings and goals. If the relationship is purely platonic, add a touch of passion.

Make sure each person is feeling nurtured by this friendship. Enjoy going places together, doing activities you both like as well as sharing your feelings.

If you don't restore the balance in your life, you will create unnecessary stress. To be healthy, you need to nurture your mind, body and spirit.

MOVING LINES

 Once you have restored balance and harmony in your life, you will be able to handle any problems easily and swiftly. You can succeed here more easily than you imagine.

 You will achieve your goal through restoring a sense of balance. A new perspective on your relationship will be forthcoming.

 Even when a relationship is going well, it is important to remain vigilant and ensure that all aspects of the partnership are being nurtured. Take time to communicate your needs and feelings.

 Do not get obsessive about your need to create balance. Remember to inject a sense of fun, spontaneity and mystery into the relationship. Travel, new activities and spending time outdoors will be of benefit now.

 You may need to seize the initiative in order to restore balance in this partnership. Be resolute and determined in your approach. Success is around the corner.

 Take responsibility for your own wellbeing. If there are shortcomings in the relationship, remember that you helped to create them. Consider what changes may be necessary to make the partnership more nurturing.

Ⓒ EXISTING PARTNERSHIPS   ⓩ NEW ROMANCE   Ⓝ FRIENDSHIP   ⊗ PITFALLS

16 AROUSAL

Thunder
Earth

Be passionate, whoever you are with and whatever you are doing, as this is the time to follow your heart. Express yourself freely in words, in gestures – even in song. Most important of all, get moving. Use all the aspects of your being to make that special connection with a loved one or friend.

Spice up your relationship with some zany humour, sexy undies, romantic songs or change of scenery. Go dancing, give each other a massage or have a cushion fight. Be playful and have fun.

Enjoy discovering new facets of your partner through wining and dining, singing and dancing, laughing and playing. Be spontaneous.

Lighten up this friendship. Inject some enthusiasm and vitality into everyday encounters. Try a new sport, go to a concert, learn to dance or visit a gym. Get moving.

Don't burn yourself out through unaccustomed physical activity. Make sure you don't overdose on hedonism or become addicted to a quick sexual thrill.

MOVING LINES

Make sure your partner or prospective partner is on the same wavelength. Don't place sexual demands on someone who would prefer a platonic relationship.

The secret of success is correct timing. There is a time for passion and a time for logic. Choose the right moment for your encounter.

There is a hidden fear here, which can result in a missed opportunity. Address your fears, overcome them and seize the right moment. If you're hesitating about asking someone out, forget your nerves and just go for it. You will be pleasantly surprised by the outcome.

You can enjoy this time of exuberance, play and passion with like-minded people. Your social life flourishes and you attract more attention from admirers than usual.

Something or someone is blocking your ability to express your passion. This is for the best, as it will prevent your feelings being abused. Try to keep your innermost thoughts to yourself at this time.

You have the opportunity to view an old passion in a new light. Don't judge yourself too harshly if you realize mistakes have been made. Once you've learned the lesson, you can then move on to more fulfilling relationships.

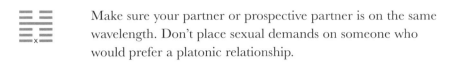

Ⓞ EXISTING PARTNERSHIPS   ⊘ NEW ROMANCE   ⓦ FRIENDSHIP   ⊗ PITFALLS

17 GO WITH THE FLOW

Lake
Thunder

This is a time to follow your intuition and let life flow. Imagine yourself as an emotional surfer riding the high waves and maintaining your balance as the wave decreases. Self-acceptance and forgiveness will help you remain centred.

 Your outer relationship reflects the inner you. This is a good time to meditate, grow spiritually and develop your intuition. Enjoy the daily ebb and flow of your relationship.

 It's too early to predict the outcome of this relationship, but have fun as you ride the emotional highs and lows.

 You can develop this friendship further by letting it blossom in its own time. Make sure your own motives are genuine and you'll benefit from this opportunity to strengthen the relationship.

 Don't push a person who is not ready to get involved in a relationship with you. If you try to cling on to someone who wishes to leave, you will cause yourself heartache. Find true happiness within.

MOVING LINES

 Don't shut the world out. You can strengthen this partnership by making sure you don't become isolated from friends and family. Make sure you plan to see friends on a regular basis – don't leave your meetings to chance.

 Do your friends share your interests? It's time to focus on developing more ties with people who share your passions and concerns. If need be, explore new places, groups or classes, as this will help to widen your social circle.

 As you develop new friendships with like-minded people, you will find old friends gradually moving away from you. Accept this natural process of change gracefully.

 Is the basis of this relationship true friendship and respect? Make sure your partner shares your sincerity and integrity; otherwise you're setting the stage for emotional stagnation.

 This is a time to count your blessings. Sincere friends and loving partners can help you make the most of your life. Enjoy focusing on the moment.

 You might have decided that you had no time for romance or more friends, but this new person in your life will change that perception. Enjoy sharing your life with someone who understands the inner you.

18 HEALING SPACE

Mountain
Wind

This is a time to look within and discover why you have not attracted into your life the love, support and care you seek. It is a wonderful opportunity to release old negative thought patterns and limiting beliefs. Remember – you deserve to love and be loved for who you are, not for what you do.

Some aspect of this relationship needs attention. Do not blame the other person if you feel unsatisfied. Look within and change your view of yourself.

Does this new relationship feel familiar? Often we simply repeat old patterns with new people until we are ready to learn the correct lesson.

This friendship is a mirror, which is reflecting some part of you that needs healing. Analyze what is going on, then take the right steps to remedy the situation.

Don't feel sorry for yourself and remain stuck in a familiar role. You can change your emotional patterns easily and joyfully once you accept the need for a new response.

MOVING LINES

 We learn patterns of happiness from our parents. It is time you reviewed what and who makes you happy. You have a chance to increase your capacity for joy.

 Have you been mothering your mate or friend? You need to develop a more equal and mutually supportive relationship. Be gentle with the other person, as they may want time to adapt.

 In your eagerness to improve your relationships you have issued an ultimatum. You have achieved the right result, but the process would have been less painful if you had been more gentle.

 You are ignoring the warning signs in this relationship. If you continue to avoid this problem, it will cause you great pain. Pay more attention to any inner feelings of unease.

 You have identified a key problem in this relationship but feel unable to address it alone. Seek the help of family, friends or a counsellor. Be gentle with yourself as you embark on the process of self-discovery.

 This is a time of inner development. Whether you are in a relationship or not, you can explore new ways to be more loving and caring to those around you. Have fun plumbing the depths and exploring the heights of your inner being.

19 WINDOW OF OPPORTUNITY

Earth
Lake

There is an opportunity to create wonderful new relationships and add emotional depth to existing ones. Make sure you use this time to build firm foundations that will survive the bad times as well as the good ones.

 You can renew your initial sense of joy, excitement and passion. Enjoy a new sense of vibrancy and vitality in this relationship.

 This is a great time to meet someone special and strengthen your relationship. Use this period to develop mutually acceptable goals and strategies that can last a lifetime.

 If you've been meaning to discuss a certain issue with your friend but have held back due to fear, go for it.

 Make sure you use this time well. Beware of fair-weather friends and partnerships based on lust rather than love. Spend time resolving any niggling issues in old relationships as well as developing new ones. Don't neglect your family.

MOVING LINES

Your popularity is increasing and you feel more attractive and outgoing. Enjoy this sensation, but be discriminating about your choice of intimate friends and partners. This is a great time to add to your circle of friends and to explore new activities that enhance your ability to enjoy life.

Respect and value yourself; then the people you attract into your life will enhance your emotional wellbeing and physical vitality. If necessary, seek independent counselling to help you boost your self-esteem and learn to release past disappointments.

Don't play power games with your loved ones or take their support for granted. You will lose their respect. Instead, take steps to boost your own confidence and inner strength.

This is a time to show your loving and caring side. You can create a warm and supportive circle of friends. Spend more time on your personal relationships and focus less on material issues.

A sense of discernment and a greater level of detachment will enable you to increase your emotional wellbeing. If need be, go on a personal development course, seek advice from an independent counsellor or spend more time outside in natural surroundings.

You have learned the lessons of love the hard way – through trial and error. Now you can enjoy the fruits of your emotional experience. Any relationship you are in at present can benefit from your growing compassion and understanding.

◎ EXISTING PARTNERSHIPS   ⊘ NEW ROMANCE   ⓪ FRIENDSHIP   ⊗ PITFALLS

20 MEDITATION

觀見

Wind
Earth

You have done everything necessary to make the best of your current situation. Now sit back, spend time relaxing and concentrate on developing detachment. Provided you have been true to yourself, you will pass this test with flying colours.

You don't have to change the person you are with to change what you get out of a relationship. If you feel stale and jaded, go within and identify those areas where you are not living up to your potential.

A new relationship allows you to see new facets of your character. Seize this chance to broaden your outlook – look at who you are and what you can deliver.

Friendships can be safe and secure places to explore your potential. Try developing new skills or going on personal development courses with your friend.

Remember: every action creates a reaction. Meditating will change your perspective and give you the chance for a fresh approach. Abandon your fear; wait for circumstances to change. Wait – it isn't time to act yet.

MOVING LINES

 You have recently come across a source of insight and wisdom, yet you are ignoring it. Take time to learn more about this alternative approach – then you can integrate it into your life.

 Too much introspection can be harmful if it simply feeds the ego. Regain a sense of perspective about your life and problems. Count your blessings.

 You realize that you are the creator of your own reality. It's time to create higher, more loving thoughts so you can attract more fulfilment into your life. Visualize the relationship you seek, believe you deserve this partnership and open your heart to welcome the right person into your life.

 Don't allow yourself to be pushed into having a role in other people's dramas. Focus on developing your own potential and allow others to find their own path. Be single-minded, detached and more discerning.

 You have the potential to inspire and heal your loved ones and associates. Stay true to yourself and continue to develop your gifts. Do not cut yourself off from the outside world while you are involved in this period of introspection.

 You know the importance of focusing on loving and positive thoughts. Try to make sure that all your actions reflect your most highly cherished values.

◐ EXISTING PARTNERSHIPS   ∅ NEW ROMANCE   ◐ FRIENDSHIP   ⊗ PITFALLS

21 BREAK THROUGH OBSTACLES

Flame
Thunder

There is an obstacle preventing this relationship from flourishing, and it can't be overcome by mere words or forceful action. Instead, it needs to be addressed through a measured series of logical steps.

 You can improve this partnership immensely by calmly and firmly identifying and addressing the problems you share. You need to agree a strategy to resolve the issue.

 The way ahead is temporarily blocked. Discover the facts of the situation and then agree a plan of action to overcome the difficulties.

 This friendship is stale at present. It can be revived with honesty and sincerity, and only if both parties are willing to change.

 When faced with an obstacle, we often run away from fear or overreact angrily. The problem here can be overcome, but only if you combine logic and intuition with assertiveness.

MOVING LINES

This situation is easily resolved by swift action. You can prevent the problem becoming overwhelming by addressing it now. Visualize the outcome you desire and then work out your steps to success. Don't delay, as the time to resolve this issue is now.

When people get angry they tend to overreact. However, anger indicates that someone has hurt you deeply, so it is better to vent your feelings than remain passive. It may help to channel some of your energy into physical activity such as t'ai chi or into creative endeavours like painting or writing.

This is a difficult issue to resolve, as the other person may be unwilling to accept responsibility for their actions and try to shift the blame on to you. Stick to your convictions.

There are genuine obstacles to this relationship. These can be resolved over time if you are prepared to invest considerable effort and persist despite any set-backs that may occur.

To resolve this obstacle you need to shoulder your fair share of blame. Change your attitude and then you will be in a strong position to discover the steps needed to improve matters.

You seem unwilling to recognize the hurdles you face. If you continue to ignore them, they will grow. Find someone to trust and discuss your frustrations with them. By bringing your anxiety out into the open, you can begin to find the source of the problem and (more importantly) a way to overcome this negative situation.

ⓞ EXISTING PARTNERSHIPS　　ⓩ NEW ROMANCE　　ⓝ FRIENDSHIP　　⊗ PITFALLS

Mountain

Flame

On the surface this relationship appears to have plenty of plus factors. There is a natural attraction and you feel a sense of wellbeing in this person's company. However, you need to check to discover whether you are compatible in fundamental ways. Do you share the same goals, for example?

Are there deep-seated differences which need to be addressed? It is often easy to remain within your comfort zone and ignore crucial issues. Enjoy the relationship for what it gives you now, but you may need to look elsewhere for long-term fulfilment.

Have fun and enjoy your new romance. If you are looking for long-term commitment, you may need to find someone whose goals are more in line with yours.

Here's a friend for the good times in life. This may not be the best person if you need a shoulder to cry on.

Don't be misled by outward appearances. This relationship may be fun, but it probably lacks the vital ingredients for a long-term commitment.

MOVING LINES

You appear to be on the receiving end of an offer that looks too good to be true. It is. Go your own way on this matter and you will eventually succeed. Do not listen to friends or family, who are only aware of a small part of the overall picture.

Physical attraction and mutual interests are not enough to sustain a relationship. Pay attention to your intuition and feelings. They have a message for you. If you feel uncomfortable in any way, take steps to explore that feeling and address any hidden issues you uncover.

Enjoy this relationship and allow your feelings to grow. Make sure that you communicate your needs and emotions clearly, as well as listening to the other person.

There appears to be a choice between two people or two routes. Look beyond the immediate attraction and pick the person or situation that will provide long-term stability and fulfilment.

You can create a warm and loving relationship. You do deserve to have emotional fulfilment. Boost your self-esteem and take the initiative in this relationship.

Here, inner reality and external circumstances match. What seems on the surface to be the right relationship for you actually is deeply rewarding and nurturing for the long term.

◐ EXISTING PARTNERSHIPS   ② NEW ROMANCE   ◑ FRIENDSHIP   ⊗ PITFALLS

23 COLLAPSE

Mountain
Earth

This is a time of endings. A relationship has run its natural course and is now in the process of disintegration. There is no point trying to save something which has reached a natural conclusion.

 Either some aspect of your partnership or the relationship itself is in the process of fundamental change. Wait and see how events unfold.

 A relationship is ending, not beginning. The dramas you may have had about this person will prove illusory.

 This friendship is destined to be changed irrevocably. The best interests of one or other party are not being served here and the situation is fundamentally unstable.

 We often feel scared and uncomfortable with endings. However, try to avoid clinging to the past, as this will make the process of moving on more difficult and stressful.

MOVING LINES

 The relationship is destabilized by a third party. Beware of gossip, jealousy and any offers by outsiders to help you resolve matters. You are the best guide here. An attempt by a so-called friend to give you useful advice could prove disastrous.

 This is a time of damage limitation. Stick to your principles and try not to overreact to events. Avoid arguments and angry confrontations. If necessary, take time out from this partnership and try to delay any important decisions until circumstances have become calmer.

 You will find the inner strength to resolve this situation. You benefit from taking a firm stand and sticking to your principles, even if the other person is not prepared to agree with you.

 An unpleasant breakup is in sight. Both parties appear to suffer, but in the long term you have a chance to find true love elsewhere. Do not be tempted to cling to an old love. Remember that this partnership was far from perfect and don't deceive yourself into thinking that the problems involved in the relationship could be resolved in the future.

 There is a chance to resolve this disagreement successfully. A satisfactory solution will be reached – this will be beneficial for both parties in the long term.

The process of disintegration has reached its natural conclusion and the seeds of a new, better way of relating have been sown. The future looks bright. Get out more and meet new people.

Ⓞ EXISTING PARTNERSHIPS ⊘ NEW ROMANCE ⓪ FRIENDSHIP ⊗ PITFALLS

24 REUNION

Earth
Thunder

The problems that prevented this relationship from flourishing have been resolved and it is time for a fresh start. You need to treat each other with care and tenderness. It takes patience and trust to rebuild a relationship.

 You have been through a rocky situation, which could have ended your partnership. Now you have the chance to build a stronger and more passionate relationship.

 If you've just met an old flame, this time you have the chance to create a meaningful relationship. Take things easily and do not force the pace.

 This is a time to renew old friendships and put them on a more realistic basis. Learn from the past and do not repeat old patterns.

 Put the past behind you, learn from your mistakes and try to avoid apportioning blame to your partner. Do not rush into a long-term commitment: let intimacy grow gradually.

MOVING LINES

 Another person may be tempting you, but you quickly realize what you have to lose by acting on a whim. You remain faithful and your existing relationship flourishes.

 You may have considered having (or have had) a brief fling, but this helps you to see that your existing partnership is the right one for you. Start spending more time with your current mate. Try praising their good qualities rather than focusing on their shortcomings.

 You always seem to imagine that life would be easier with a different partner. Try changing your own attitudes rather than swapping partners. If necessary, consider some counselling or a workshop on self-development. You have the key to your own happiness.

 Mistakes have been made in the past and you have chosen ill-advisedly. Now you have a new determination to choose someone who shares your long-term goals. Take your time and don't rush headlong into a new relationship.

 Forgiveness is the key to resolving the differences that have arisen here. With compassion and mutual understanding, this relationship can be repaired if you want it to succeed.

 If you ignore this opportunity to rebuild your relationship, you will not be given a second chance. Look within and consider your options carefully. Once you have decided, there is no going back.

◑ EXISTING PARTNERSHIPS   ② NEW ROMANCE   ◍ FRIENDSHIP   ⊗ PITFALLS

25 PURITY OF INTENT

Heaven
Thunder

The key to this situation is to treat the other person the same way you would like to be treated if you were in their position. The situation is quite clear-cut. Your confusion will disappear once you stop playing emotional games and speak your truth.

 Be honest with each other. Agree a set of parameters for your relationship to flourish within, and stick with them. Do not compromise your principles.

 You need to do some plain talking and establish some firm guidelines. Then this relationship can proceed smoothly.

 Are you being honest with each other? Are certain subjects deliberately avoided? You can improve this relationship by communicating your needs and feelings clearly.

 Make sure you know exactly how you feel and what you want from this relationship before you start discussing its future. Be honest with yourself.

MOVING LINES

Listen to your heart and follow your instincts. You can achieve the intimacy and commitment you seek. You need to be the leader here. Spend more quality time with your partner – and don't worry about the consequences of sharing your deepest thoughts with another.

Make sure you do not override your feelings. Trust your instincts on a daily basis and do not ignore small signs of stress. You may need to adjust your own behaviour in order to obtain the emotional satisfaction you seek from your mate.

Even though you've been honest and open, your partner has fallen short of these standards in some way. Learn what you can from the situation and don't dwell on it. Your next relationship will be more rewarding.

Be confident that you have the right set of relationships you need at the moment. Don't chase after someone who clearly doesn't wish to be with you. If you choose to pursue another partner on a whim, you will suffer in the short and long term.

In times of difficulty, you need to assess whether you contributed to the situation in any way. If you didn't, just sit tight and matters will improve. Spend some time on yourself.

Now is not the time for action, however sincere you are. Any attempts to resolve the situation at this time will be counter-productive and unsuccessful. Be patient and wait for a more fortuitous occasion to make your move.

---

① EXISTING PARTNERSHIPS   ② NEW ROMANCE   ⑩ FRIENDSHIP   ⊗ PITFALLS

26 SOUL MATE

Mountain
Heaven

This relationship could well evolve into a long-term commitment. There is a special chemistry: you share the same basic beliefs and values in life. The sense of a shared perspective can nourish and support you both in times of joy and sorrow.

 Stick with this relationship. Through this partnership you can uncover hidden emotional depths and develop your full potential.

 If you are just looking for a fling, beware – this relationship has staying power! Be prepared to get serious.

 A sign of true friendship. This person will remain a source of support and companionship throughout your life if you wish.

 There is a sense of destiny about this relationship. Pay attention to your boundaries and don't allow yourself to be swamped by the other person. Make sure you keep your outside interests and stay in touch with friends and family.

MOVING LINES

 Don't rush into this relationship headlong, as there is an obstacle which needs to be overcome. Identify the difficulty and devise a strategy to resolve the issue. Then take your time to initiate your plan; success is then assured.

 It's definitely not the time to get involved with this person or to try to further the relationship. Spend quality time with yourself, your friends and your family. If necessary, learn a new skill or join a health club.

 There is potential for happiness here, but the way forward is tricky. You will need to overcome a series of hurdles. Be patient and persistent in your approach. Do not allow small set-backs to deter you from your long-term goals.

 You need to take action to prevent a minor issue turning into a major headache. Act now and you can successfully nip it in the bud. Be ruthless and do not indulge in half measures.

 You should try to encourage your partner to develop some outside interests. Otherwise, too much aggression and energy will be directed at you. Take care of your physical safety and emotional stability.

 Now is the time to cement this partnership. All of the obstacles have been cleared away. Go for your heart's desire: celebrate your relationship with a romantic weekend holiday, a night of unbridled passion or a special meal for two in your favourite restaurant.

◑ EXISTING PARTNERSHIPS   ② NEW ROMANCE   ⑩ FRIENDSHIP   ⊗ PITFALLS

27 LOOK AFTER YOURSELF

Mountain
Thunder

The key to this situation is to develop greater awareness of your own needs. As you discover how to optimize your potential, you will be able to assist your partner and friends in their process of self-fulfilment.

 Is one partner putting more effort into this relationship? In order to prosper, both of you need to feel valued, nurtured and supported.

 Is this a healthy relationship? Make sure you are not slipping into old roles, such as rescuer and victim, or knight in shining armour and damsel in distress.

 Check whether your friendship has slid into unhealthy patterns. Is one of you playing the adult; the other, the child?

 It is important to create balance in your life. This includes making sure that you eat well, sleep well, exercise, explore your creativity and go partying. You also need to balance time spent alone with time spent in other people's company.

MOVING LINES

Why are you struggling to get something or someone you don't need? You have everything you require to be happy. Don't chase after someone else's partner. Explore other ways to be creative in your life – consider painting, writing or drama, for example. The answer to this situation is within your grasp.

You are far stronger than you think and have no need to play out the role of victim in order to win love. Heal your past pain and release this unhelpful pattern of behaviour.

You seem to be chasing after an illusion. A series of quick flings is ultimately going to leave you feeling less loved. Isn't it time to invest more effort in a long-term partnership?

You are very keen to develop this relationship further, as you can see its inherent potential for success. Relax a little; you will get the love and attention you crave in due course. Timing is crucial here: you can't force the pace of this relationship, however hard you try.

This is a time for inner healing and reflection. Consider visiting a counsellor or someone whose opinion you value. Explore new ways of personal development and fresh avenues for your creativity.

Here's a relationship with great potential, which will require nurturing. You will reap many benefits, both emotionally and spiritually, from this encounter. Stick with the process even if at times you yearn for an easier ride.

Ⓞ EXISTING PARTNERSHIPS   ⓥ NEW ROMANCE   ⓦ FRIENDSHIP   ⊗ PITFALLS

28 SOUL LOVE

Lake
Wind

This is an exceptional time – your spirits can soar and you can experience a feeling of oneness with all beings. You may find your current love contrasts poorly with this ecstatic spiritual experience, so stay with your experience and trust that when the time is right your worldly relationships will also flourish.

 It might not be possible to share your feelings with your partner fully, and as a result they may feel alienated. Try to stay with the process and keep opening your heart.

 If you have just met someone and they have triggered this feeling, it's like you've been hit by a meteor. Don't make any long-term decisions at this stage.

 You may need to reassess friendships and partnerships in due course. For now, create more time and space for yourself.

 Times of extreme emotion and transformation are always difficult. In this case, the outcome is good, so long as you don't try to force the pace of the process.

MOVING LINES

 This is a time to be cautious and to explore all your options with an open mind. Don't leap into commitments. It may help to discuss your situation with close friends or family.

 There is a potential partner in your current circle who you have not yet identified. If you don't know who this person is, ask a friend to help you track them down.

 You are heading for an emotional quagmire and have only yourself to blame. It is too late to correct the situation. The sooner you head for the exit, the better. Try to get in touch with your intuition. Did you avoid listening to an inner warning as you rushed headlong into this liaison? Learn from this mistake and forgive yourself for your misjudgement.

 You are blessed with many qualities that help you to attract the partner you desire. Don't abuse your power or you'll find this situation causes you grief and stress.

 Is this relationship simply an old pattern reasserting itself? In order to grow you need to find new ways to express yourself and create relationships that allow you to flourish.

Sometimes it is important to take a stand on principle. In the short term this might lead to sorrow and the end of a relationship, but the long-term outlook is excellent.

① EXISTING PARTNERSHIPS   ② NEW ROMANCE   ⑪ FRIENDSHIP   ⊗ PITFALLS

29 POTENTIAL DANGER

Water
Water

There is a very real problem to be faced in this relationship. It's not a matter of making a psychological adjustment to a situation, but a genuine need for prompt and appropriate action. Follow your heart in this matter, as you alone have the key to unlock the door that's blocking your happiness.

 There is a genuine problem here – it is ongoing and requires you to take some difficult decisions. You will succeed if you practise tough love.

 Turn detective and try to discover more about your new partner's life. You can go on to develop this relationship further if you wish, after facing some unpalatable facts.

 Are you being dragged unwittingly into a dangerous situation through your desire to help someone? Before you agree to get involved in a mutual project or to offer your assistance, check the potential consequences.

 Face up to some unsavoury facts. If you avoid tackling the problem, it will grow and damage you emotionally. Get help from a counsellor or third party if need be.

MOVING LINES

If you put up with an uncomfortable situation for too long, you grow accustomed to it and lose the ability to change it. Don't allow yourself to make excuses about your partner.

The first thing to do here is to minimize the risk. Seek the assistance of a third party and devise a long-term strategy to resolve matters. Be vigilant here and don't be too proud to end the relationship if necessary.

This is not a time for action. The only helpful thing to do is to wait and see how the situation unfolds. Be patient and stay calm. Keep in touch with friends and family.

Go within and meditate in order to seek the emotional strength and new perspective necessary to resolve this issue. You do have the answer to this problem.

Focus on overcoming the existing obstacle in this relationship. This is not a time to try to deepen the level of commitment between the two of you.

At this moment you are unable to see your way through the problems in this relationship. Your current options are limited. Do not bury your head in the sand: seek help from an unbiased outsider.

30 ILLUMINATION

Flame
Flame

Follow your heart and learn to tune in to the cycles of the universe. Relationships are similar to flowers in that they start from a seed, blossom, then die. Learn to recognize where you are in a particular relationship and act appropriately. A new relationship requires careful nurturing; an existing one may have to be pruned; and an old one needs cutting back.

Don't take each other for granted. Take the time to reassess your relationship and see how you might create an even more wonderful partnership.

Share your visions and dreams with the other person. Explore how you might make a difference in the world.

This friendship has great possibilities and can help you to discover your true self. Encourage each other to be creative, try new forms of self-expression and have fun.

This is a wonderful time to express yourself and discover your true potential. Remember, however, that ideas and projects take time to materialize and other people's attitudes may need to change.

MOVING LINES

Pay particular attention to new beginnings in your life. How you approach a particular person the first time you meet them will determine much of what is to follow.

Here's a marvellous opportunity to develop a relationship or mutual project. You have all the emotional resources you need to enjoy this partnership. Start spending more time with this person and visualizing how the relationship could add joy, vitality and serenity to your life.

This relationship is weakening and you are drifting apart. Don't try to cling on to the other person or to end the partnership prematurely. Let it run its course and you will learn many valuable lessons. These will help you create more fulfilling relationships in the future.

This is a passionate fling that is burning itself out. The emotional intensity which fuelled this relationship has been used up. Count your blessings, remember the good times and move on.

Don't be sad if you appear to be losing touch with someone or no longer feel the same sense of passion. A new passion will develop in due course.

If you're not getting what you want from a relationship, consider finishing it. After you have done that, examine yourself and see how you can change your attitudes in order to attract more love.

Ⓞ EXISTING PARTNERSHIPS   ② NEW ROMANCE   ⑩ FRIENDSHIP   ⊗ PITFALLS

31 MUTUAL ATTRACTION

Lake
Mountain

A wonderful time is approaching if you are looking for a long-term partnership. There is a strong bond here between you and the other person. Look inside your heart and see if you are ready for commitment. If you are, now is the perfect time to accept a proposal to marry or move in together.

This partnership has what it takes to create a lasting, loving relationship. Keep putting in the time and effort to transform the initial attraction into a solid relationship.

If you have just met someone and are looking for a lifetime partner, this is great news. This person has the potential to fulfil that role for you.

Is this a friendship or is there some element of sexual attraction? Check out your feelings and, if it feels right, explore the idea of becoming more than friends.

The chief danger here is that the attraction is so strong that both parties will take it for granted. Try to establish some mutually acceptable guidelines and make sure you spend enough time together as the relationship matures.

MOVING LINES

 You have already met your potential partner, but they haven't indicated their interest in you. Stay cool.

 Don't jump into an embarrassing situation by expressing your feelings prematurely to someone – await events. Eventually you will emerge triumphant, but not perhaps in the way you initially thought.

 Don't act on the spur of the moment. Before you decide to embark on a new relationship or alter the terms of an existing one, make sure you know exactly what you want to achieve.

 If you follow your heart and express your true feelings, you will eventually find the love you seek. Don't try to manipulate those you profess to love, as that will lead to tears.

 It seems as if you are on automatic pilot. Some inner voice is dictating your every action. Go with the flow. The important thing is to seize the initiative and regain a sense of control over your own life.

 If you enjoy flirting, go ahead. At this time you can have fun and there'll be no serious or damaging consequences. Enjoy yourself and party.

32 FOLLOW YOUR OWN PATH

Thunder
Wind

Each of us has a path to take through life. It is unique and special. It is important now to keep moving at the correct rhythm along your particular life journey. Don't be distracted or pulled off your path by other people or your own negative thoughts.

 Is your partner helping you to achieve your goals? See how you feel after you've discussed these dreams with your partner. If you feel inspired, great. If you feel depressed, now is the time to heal your inner critic.

 If this new relationship involves compromising some of your goals, then think again. You deserve to realize your dreams and to have a supportive partner.

 Are you spending too much time propping up this person? Make sure your friendships are mutually supportive.

 To achieve your goals you must be focused. Make sure you don't sacrifice your dreams in order to buy love. You can have a loving relationship and fulfil your potential.

MOVING LINES

You cannot find a solution to a difficulty before you know exactly what the problem is. Take time to explore the differences between you and then take the appropriate action to resolve them.

If you stay true to yourself, you can enjoy this relationship. It may not fulfil all the aspects of your being, but it will be nurturing.

Don't allow your partner to change your basic agenda for a relationship. If you settle for second-best, you will be sorry. Keep your options open rather than agreeing to a compromise that starves you of enough emotional support.

Are you looking for love in the wrong place? If you have always been unlucky in your choice of mate, use this opportunity to change your views on what makes an ideal partner.

On this occasion if your emotions conflict with your logic then stick to the rational solution. Don't be distracted by a whim or quick fling. Analyze the facts of the situation, draw up a list of pros and cons, then make a firm decision.

Don't make any decisions in haste. Now is the time to consider your options calmly and carefully. Once you have made a choice, stick with it. If necessary, seek support from like-minded people who have experienced similar situations in the past.

◐ EXISTING PARTNERSHIPS   ⊘ NEW ROMANCE   ⊕ FRIENDSHIP   ⊗ PITFALLS

33 CREATING A BOUNDARY

Heaven
Mountain

It's time to create some inner space for yourself in this relationship. This is a difficult period – headlong confrontation is to be avoided as it would cause mutual pain. It is not, however, a time to go along with the other person's wishes and timetable.

 If you feel squashed or pushed into a corner, don't react aggressively. Be calm and firm in your refusal to go along with your partner's plans.

 Don't confuse passion with possessiveness. If the other person, through insecurity, tries to impose conditions on your behaviour, refuse in a loving way.

 It is time to reassess the amount of support you are offering your friend. Are you being taken advantage of? Learn to say no gently and firmly.

 This is a difficult situation, as there is a temptation either to ignore the problem or to overreact angrily. A slow, steady approach to disentangling some aspects of your life from this relationship is important.

MOVING LINES

At this point in time, it's best to refrain from action and appear to ignore a contentious issue. The time to act will occur in due course. In the meantime, boost your morale by spending time with friends and giving yourself a special treat.

If you try to break up this relationship, the other person will refuse to go along with your decision. There is unfinished business between you. You need to draw on your emotional resources and prepare for a lengthy process of separation.

You need to try to convince the other person that it is time for a change. They are unwilling to let you go, so you will need to negotiate some form of separation.

You will feel much better after you have decided to go your own way on this matter. However, your partner will be angry and hurt. Try not to let your emotions get entangled with theirs. Stay calm and centred.

An amicable separation can be agreed now. You will still need to be firm, but the outcome is good. You can remain friends and avoid causing each other unnecessary pain.

You know exactly what you want and how to achieve it. You can leave this situation with a smile on your face and a warm glow in your heart.

⦵ EXISTING PARTNERSHIPS ⦶ NEW ROMANCE ⦷ FRIENDSHIP ⊗ PITFALLS

34 INNER POWER

Thunder
Heaven

You have all the resources you need to discover the best solution to your current problem. However, you must be patient and pick the correct time in the future for action. It is also vital that, in your enthusiasm for a person or a project, you don't use your forceful personality to persuade someone to act temporarily in a way which is out of character. If you misuse your gifts, you will face an emotional backlash after a short while.

You can see clearly what you want, but do take time and effort to explain to your partner how your dream can be achieved. Patience will pay dividends.

The other person may not be as convinced as you are about the potential for this partnership. Visualize the outcome you desire and do not push the pace.

Hold fast to your dreams and visions. Offer these to the other person and then allow them to proceed at their own pace. Now is not the time to issue ultimatums.

When you feel something strongly and can see it clearly, it is hard to come to terms with the fact that no one else shares your vision. Time is on your side as long as you are patient.

MOVING LINES

Don't try to push the other person into a tight corner. You may have logic on your side but you can't succeed at this stage.

The way ahead is clear now. Don't overplay your hand through excess enthusiasm. You can win this person or argument, but you will need to be patient and kind.

If you get involved in this situation you will fail. The current circumstances are not conducive to change. Any effort would be like pouring water into a leaky bucket.

You can win in this situation through staying true to your beliefs and making sure all your actions are consistent with your heart's desire. Opposition will melt away without the need for harsh words.

You will be surprised at how easy it is to get what you want from this relationship now. Past opposition to your requests will evaporate. Enjoy your success.

You can't get everything you want from this relationship. However, some progress is possible. Once this is achieved you will fare best by not pressing ahead, but waiting for a more opportune time to complete the process.

Ⓒ EXISTING PARTNERSHIPS   ⓓ NEW ROMANCE   ⓝ FRIENDSHIP   ⊗ PITFALLS

35 MOVING FORWARD EASILY

Flame
Earth

This is a time of joy and ease. Together you and your partner can work towards greater intimacy and fulfilment. Honour each other's differences and don't try to force your partner to become more like you. Hold a vision of love, success and wellbeing for each other.

 Each of you has decided independently that you wish to move the relationship forward to its next stage. As you're perfectly in tune with each other, you will find events and situations unfold naturally to support your mutual decision.

 Even though you have just met, it will seem as if you have known each other for a long time. You will find it easy to establish a loving relationship.

 You'll find new areas to explore together. The friendship can deepen and strengthen as you share your feelings and aspirations with each other.

 Make sure that you don't dominate your partner. Continued success depends on a shared vision, rather than you simply imposing your dreams on the other person.

MOVING LINES

If you have a suggestion to make to your partner or would like to ask someone out, go ahead. Even if they do not agree, there will be no regrets, and you will discover something which will be of great value to you in the future.

There is something or someone temporarily preventing you from getting in touch with the person you seek. Now is not the time to try to force the issue. You will succeed at a later date.

You need to enlist the help of your friends to secure an introduction to a new person in your life. Don't be afraid to ask for help from others. Success is in sight.

Don't play fast and loose with another person's affections. If you opt for a quick fling, you will be the ultimate loser and your reputation will suffer.

Even though this is a wonderful time to create a new relationship, don't get upset if no suitable suitor appears. Stay true to your feelings and you will find the happiness you seek.

There is a feeling now that you can take on the world, and that would be a mistake. Focus on creating more harmony and nurturing close to home, rather than boldly trying to form new relationships.

◐ EXISTING PARTNERSHIPS　　② NEW ROMANCE　　⓪ FRIENDSHIP　　⊗ PITFALLS

36 EMOTIONAL SHIELD

Earth
Flame

This is a difficult time. You will meet opposition in your relationships, either from unhelpful outsiders or from the inner demons of your partner. You can't change matters now. Instead, you need to protect yourself by building your self-esteem and avoid energy-sapping conflicts.

 Keep your thoughts and feelings to yourself. Be selfish and focus on your own needs. Take care of the basics: good food, exercise and a sound night's sleep. See your friends to help keep your spirits high.

 There's a clash of values here. Stay true to yourself and don't get bogged down by someone else's negative feelings.

 This is an unhealthy situation. You may wish to consider how to reduce your contact with this person. In any event, you need to put your needs first and find other like-minded people to assist you at this time.

 The danger here is that you will be overwhelmed by the other person's negativity. Do whatever is necessary to keep your morale high and your physical energy flowing. You may need to go off by yourself for a while.

MOVING LINES

Unfortunately, you will need to go it alone at this time. Your partner will not support the stance you have adopted, but you can gain the help you need from a friend or family member.

You can see clearly that there is a dangerous situation which is likely to affect you and your partner adversely. Your partner is unable to recognize the danger at this time, so keep pointing out the likely pitfalls.

You resolve this situation easily – almost too easily. Remember: this problem has a long history and your partner will find it hard to act in new ways. Patience!

You can gain a greater insight now into the problem which besets this relationship. Having faced up to the issue, you see that it's insuperable at present. Consider cutting your losses and seeking love elsewhere.

It is not the right time to leave this partnership. The only way to handle such a tricky situation is to keep your own counsel and develop friendships outside the relationship.

A period of depression is over for you. It seemed that something dreadful was about to befall you and then suddenly you were released from the relationship. Move on joyfully.

Ⓞ EXISTING PARTNERSHIPS   ⊘ NEW ROMANCE   ⑩ FRIENDSHIP   ⊗ PITFALLS

37 THE WORLD IN MINIATURE

Wind
Flame

R elationships are a wonderful way of exploring our
true selves and developing our character. Many people
rush around seeking a spiritual path to follow, when each
and every relationship they choose to be in represents part
of their path. At this time your greatest lesson is wrapped
up in this relationship.

This partnership is a magnificent opportunity for you to learn
more about the balance between logic and emotions. Recognize
and accept your feelings, but let your rational side dictate
whether or not you choose to act on short-lived emotions.

There is a good reason why this relationship has come into
your life. Do you have difficulty expressing your feelings?
Have you suppressed your own potential in order not to
threaten someone else's comfort zone? Now is the chance
to gain a new sense of harmony.

This is a challenging friendship, where you need to be aware
of your boundaries and balance your needs with those of
your friend.

Each of us has the answers to all our problems within. Use this relationship to deepen your connection with your own inner wisdom, not as a prop for your ego.

MOVING LINES

 It is important to take charge of your own thinking process. Negative thoughts, perhaps developed when you were a child, need to be eradicated. Try some positive affirmations.

 How you treat yourself will be mirrored by how others treat you. If you are unhappy about some aspect of a relationship, start by giving yourself what you're seeking from the other person.

 Sometimes we have to give up some instant gratification for a longer-term gain. Don't fool yourself into accepting second-best.

 Follow your heart and instincts on this matter. You and you alone are the best guide at the moment.

 Trying to understand another's feelings is not going to help here. You need to pay attention both to what you are told and to the other person's actual behaviour. Logic, not emotion, is the key.

 You can resolve any difficulties you may face through going within, releasing other people's expectations and opening your heart. The answer will come through inner focus.

ⓞ EXISTING PARTNERSHIPS   ⓔ NEW ROMANCE   ⓝ FRIENDSHIP   ⊗ PITFALLS

38 OPPOSITES ATTRACT

Flame
Lake

Sometimes conflict can be revitalizing and thought-provoking. This relationship could work in the short term, so long as you both respect the other's point of view, but it is difficult (though not impossible) to create a successful long-term relationship where the underlying values and beliefs vary so dramatically.

This is a challenging partnership. You need to recognize that there are certain areas where agreement is unlikely. Only you can decide how important these areas are to you.

Enjoy this relationship for what it can offer and don't try to predict its outcome. Learn to live in the moment.

This is a complex friendship, where your values on some issues clash drastically. Don't alter your behaviour or try to change the other person. Learn instead to accommodate the differences.

The danger here is that you will let your emotions override your logic. Don't ignore the differences in long-term goals or philosophies of life.

MOVING LINES

 You can't resolve the difficulties in this relationship through direct action. The other person needs time to decide on their own how they wish to proceed. Learn to trust.

 You appear to be at loggerheads with your partner. An unexpected turn of events or the intervention of a third party will provide the opportunity for reconciliation.

 This relationship has got off to a bad start. All you can see are obstacles at every turn. Relax. The outcome is good, so long as you don't have a rush of blood to the head and say something hurtful to the other person out of anger.

 In the past you may have found it difficult to meet like-minded people, but that is about to change. You can share your life with someone who holds the same values and beliefs as you.

 You have already met your perfect partner, but you haven't yet recognized them as your true love. Be patient, as their identity will be revealed shortly. In the meantime, focus on being positive and upbeat.

 You appear to have badly misjudged someone. Are you scared of commitment? Give them a chance to prove that they are trustworthy, loving and loyal. Release your fear of intimacy and allow this new romance to flourish. You deserve to enjoy a close, loving relationship and you do have the emotional maturity to create a fulfilling partnership.

⟲ EXISTING PARTNERSHIPS   ⊘ NEW ROMANCE   ⟲ FRIENDSHIP   ⊗ PITFALLS

39 RELEASE OLD PATTERNS

Water
Mountain

This can be rather an exasperating time, as relationships seem to be going through a difficult patch. The key is to transform your own negative thoughts and release outdated patterns of behaviour. This may be easier and more fun to do with like-minded people – perhaps through a workshop or course of counselling.

 You can overcome the difficulties you face by changing your attitude. Avoid blaming your partner and concentrate on being more positive.

 See this relationship as an opportunity to create lasting and valuable change rather than as a problem. The time is right for you to boost your self-esteem and open your heart.

 Don't give up on this friendship because it feels uncomfortable. Learn to be more caring and compassionate.

 Avoid running away from your problems. You now have a genuine opportunity to clear past trauma and create a supportive relationship.

MOVING LINES

 This is not the right time to address the problem you face. Don't ignore it totally: simply avoid direct confrontation until a later date. You'll know when the time is right to discuss this issue and will be glad that you were patient.

 Tough as it may be, you need to face this difficulty head on. Do not delay and don't let other people weaken your determination to resolve the issue. If necessary, seek help from friends or family.

 It is your turn either to apologize or give in gracefully to the wishes of your partner. You can enjoy a passionate reconciliation if you are sincere in your apology and prepared to back up your words with new patterns of behaviour.

 You have insufficient information to resolve this issue. You need to find support from friends or experts in this type of problem. This will give you the advice and support you require to tackle this question successfully.

 Here you play the role of teacher and it's a chance to help your partner overcome some difficulty. Get as much support from friends and family as you can. Do not feel overwhelmed: you have the necessary emotional resources to handle this situation successfully.

 Don't give up on the idea of creating a successful relationship. The prospects for the current partnership are good if you use wisely all the emotional resources you've developed.

⦿ EXISTING PARTNERSHIPS   ⊘ NEW ROMANCE   ⦾ FRIENDSHIP   ⊗ PITFALLS

40 FORGIVENESS

Thunder
Water

This is a time to forgive yourself and your partner. The difficulties you faced are now being resolved. Try to get back to a steady emotional keel now. Don't boast about your recent success in persuading your partner to agree to your terms.

 It is hard not to brag when success comes after a series of obstacles have been overcome. The sooner you forget the recent fracas and move on, the better the prospects for your partnership.

 You have survived some traumatic times, and calmer emotional shores are in sight. Enjoy this period, but do not boast about your romantic conquest.

 The tension between you is easing and a new way of relating needs to emerge. Try to avoid reprimanding the other person or drawing their attention to past mistakes.

 The danger here is that in your elation you will set up a backlash of resentment. Be gracious in victory and happy to focus on the present.

MOVING LINES

 This is a time to relax and enjoy each other's company. Set aside plenty of time to be alone with each other and rediscover your romance and passion. If possible, go away for a romantic weekend or recreate your first meeting.

 Don't use a sledgehammer to crack a nut. The worst of your problems are over and you can handle the remaining issues calmly and confidently. Spend some time visualizing a greater sense of peace and harmony, rather than mentally rehearsing your arguments.

 You are not invincible. It may feel wonderful to have successfully resolved an old problem, but this doesn't mean you now have a magic wand which can change a friend into a partner.

 While you were going through a difficult time with your partner, you became close to some people with whom you have little in common. It is now time to refocus on your partner.

 You have the power within to free yourself from this problematic relationship. You deserve to have a fulfilling relationship. Take whatever steps are necessary to secure a loving future.

 You are prepared and ready to act. What is stopping you? You'll be successful if you take swift, appropriate action to end this time of emotional hardship. Remember – you do have the ability to create more joy and happiness in your life. Don't settle for second-best.

◎ EXISTING PARTNERSHIPS   ∅ NEW ROMANCE   ◍ FRIENDSHIP   ⊗ PITFALLS

41 LETTING GO

Mountain
Lake

When love is over, it's best to let go with grace. If you get angry and try to convince or cajole the other person into staying with you, you'll simply prolong the pain. This is a time to draw on your inner resources. Try to part as friends, not foes.

 This relationship is under pressure. Are you fulfilled at present? If not, be brave and take steps to discover a new partner.

 This romance doesn't seem destined to blossom into true love. Don't despair if it fails to get off the ground, as someone better will show up in the future.

 This friendship is gradually ending. There may have been great closeness in the past but circumstances have changed now. You'll start moving in different social circles.

 Don't feel angry or sad when a relationship ends. This is a chance for self-development, so take those courses you always planned to do when you had time. Be creative, be artistic and learn new skills.

MOVING LINES

Don't take advantage of someone who loves you more than you care for them. Be honest about your intentions. This will cause less pain in the long run and will ensure that your partner does not become hostile or violent.

True love doesn't mean sacrificing yourself on the altar of another person's ego. Stay true to yourself. Do not put all your dreams on hold in order to boost your partner's self-esteem.

If you're locked in a love triangle, be warned – it will quickly fall apart. Don't accept second-best. If you decide to leave, you'll be able to find a suitable partner who is prepared to be committed solely to you.

Try being less critical of yourself and others. Be willing to explore relationships with people who are not normally your type. Experiment and have fun. Try to look beyond external appearances and explore mutual goals and values.

You are destined to meet your true love and enjoy a mutually satisfying relationship. Trust that your perfect partner will arrive at the appropriate moment.

Use the wisdom and understanding you've developed to help others repair their relationships. Share your joy and happiness with friends and family. You may become a mentor to another family member, who is wrestling with relationship difficulties.

⓪ EXISTING PARTNERSHIPS   ② NEW ROMANCE   ⑩ FRIENDSHIP   ⊗ PITFALLS

LOVE BLOSSOMS

Wind
Thunder

This is a very special time, when love can deepen and you can create a lasting bond with your partner. Use this time wisely and you can reap the benefit from it for the rest of your life.

 A great time to move in together, get married or conceive a child. This is an opportunity for greater intimacy, passion and mutual understanding.

 You have a chance to establish a lasting bond with this person very quickly. This is not simply a quick fling. If you are looking for a lifetime partner, you have just won the jackpot.

 Is this merely a friendship or something more? There is an opportunity here to move the relationship towards a romantic partnership. Check it out.

 Take advantage of this wonderful period while you can. Make sure you share your good fortune with friends and families, as your joy can help inspire and motivate others.

MOVING LINES

You now have the support and stability you need to make your dreams come true. Use your new confidence and vitality wisely. Identify your mutual goals and devise a strategy for obtaining each one.

Enjoy the love and happiness you are currently experiencing. Don't take your partner for granted. Get to know your in-laws and extended family better. Spend more time on your relationship and reassess the amount of energy you pour into work commitments.

Sometimes it takes real problems to make us realize how truly blessed we are. You have a wonderful partner, who will help you overcome your current difficulties. Learn to confide your deepest fears and you will realize your worries are transitory.

Are you spoiling the one you love? Are you playing hard to get? Forget the games; this is an opportunity for a genuine loving relationship. Go for it. Open your heart, be honest with yourself and your partner.

The way to resolve your difficulty is to treat the other person the way you would like to be treated. Try to be kind and considerate. Success will follow so long as you are honest, sincere and compassionate.

Are you playing the field? That is no way to discover true love. If you want a faithful, loyal mate you need to be ready to stick to one partner. It is your decision. Think it over.

◐ EXISTING PARTNERSHIPS   ② NEW ROMANCE   ◑ FRIENDSHIP   ⊗ PITFALLS

43 RESOLUTION

Lake
Heaven

The tension that has been building up in your love life over a particular person or issue is on the verge of being released. You can see clearly now what needs to be done to resolve matters. Be logical and take the appropriate action.

Now is not the time to compromise. You know in your heart what is the right course of action. Do it now.

If you have just met someone new, they have the answer to your emotional conundrum. You will gain a new clarity, and this will help you to identify the correct course of action.

Have you been trying to gloss over a problem? Have you resorted to half-truths and omissions? Now is the time to be honest and open, even if it means ending the relationship.

Look into your heart, make sure you know what you want and go for it. The time for half measures is past. If you don't take a stand now, you'll regret the missed opportunity later and only increase your heartache.

MOVING LINES

Now that you have identified a way forward, take it one step at a time. There is still a missing factor you need to discover if you are to ensure a smooth transition.

If you have prepared the ground and resolved your own emotional conflicts, then all will be well. Don't give out mixed messages or you'll create more pain. Stick to your decision and don't give your partner any more chances.

It is not yet the time to make your move, even though outsiders will criticize you for being weak or indecisive. Follow your heart: you'll know when the time is ripe to issue your ultimatum.

You would like matters to be resolved right now, if not yesterday. There is no point pushing at the moment. Try to be patient. There is another person involved in this issue.

You've made your decision, so don't waiver. Stick to your logical assessment of what is in your best interests. Don't let passing sadness or moments of lust stop you from making the break. Do it now.

You think you have resolved matters, but deep within is a seed of doubt – could it have worked out? If you allow this seed to flourish, you'll put yourself in a very traumatic position.

◐ EXISTING PARTNERSHIPS   ② NEW ROMANCE   ◑ FRIENDSHIP   ⊗ PITFALLS

44 POTENTIAL PITFALLS

Heaven
Wind

You need to be on your guard here. An old flame or
negative emotional pattern is reappearing in your life.
There is still some unfinished business. If you don't want to
experience an emotional quagmire, take this opportunity
to root out your negative thoughts about love and intimacy.

Does your relationship seem to go in phases? Do you
recognize the start of a downward cycle? Use this awareness
to change the old pattern.

This may be someone new, but the relationship has all the
hallmarks of past failures. Change your way of thinking.

You may have thought you'd resolved the outstanding matters
between you and the other person, but your friend will test
your mettle. Be tough if necessary.

It's very easy to slip back into old painful patterns and return
to old partners. This means you need to heal that part of
yourself which believes you don't deserve a loving and
fulfilling relationship.

MOVING LINES

If you let this situation run its course, you'll have a major problem on your hands. Act quickly to nip this in the bud. Do whatever it takes to end this relationship once and for all.

There is no need to issue an ultimatum. If you remain firm and stick to your principles, you can effectively manage this situation without it blowing up into a row. Time is on your side.

You would prefer to go along with the other person's views, even though you do not agree with them. Circumstances will intervene and you'll have an ideal opportunity to express your opposition.

Try not to leave any bad blood between you. Be gentle and firm. The other person may try to cling to the past, but don't let them cling to you.

At present, it may not seem as if you can win, but you will. Your views will be accepted willingly in due course. Sit tight, wait and see how events conspire to bring you everything you wished for.

If you stick to your principles, you may find yourself without a mate. If you give in, you'll be bruised emotionally. Follow your heart and prepare for future success elsewhere in a healthier, more stable and supportive relationship.

45 MEETING OF HEARTS

Lake
Earth

This is an inspiring time, when relationships can grow and flourish. But it is important not to neglect your own personal development. Beware of losing your identity within the partnership: do not sacrifice your goals for those of the other person.

You have a magnificent opportunity to create a deep relationship here. The only concern is that you will be deprived of an opportunity to excel in some way. Make sure you continue to explore your creativity and interests outside the relationship.

Here's a great chance to create the perfect partnership. Don't compromise on anything vital to you in the flush of passion. You deserve happiness and personal growth.

You don't have to swap friendships for compliance with the other person's wishes. Spend more time developing your own talents and gifts.

Danger – in your desire for closeness with another person you will lose sight of your own needs and potential.

MOVING LINES

This relationship is worth pursuing. Do not listen to gossips or misguided friends who will try to influence your decision. Follow your heart and explore the potential for passion in this partnership.

It will feel as if you have known this person all your life. Now is the right time for this partnership. The relationship will develop effortlessly. Enjoy yourself as you create a stable foundation for a long-term love.

Is the object of your desire available? If not, it would be better to turn your attention elsewhere. There is a potential partner in your existing social circle. Don't be tempted to settle for being one member of a triangle.

A genuine love match. You can enhance each other's emotional wellbeing and provide the support necessary for you both to succeed in the outside world. Celebrate your love with spontaneity and joy.

A third party may try to interfere in this relationship. People are often attracted by what they can't have. Stay true to your partner and don't be tempted to have a fling.

You are interested in having a relationship with someone but they misunderstand your approach. All is not lost. In due course, you can establish a successful partnership with this person.

◐ EXISTING PARTNERSHIPS ⌀ NEW ROMANCE ◑ FRIENDSHIP ⊗ PITFALLS

46 WORTH THE EFFORT

Earth
Wind

Y ou can achieve the progress you desire in this
relationship. However, you must be single-minded and
work relentlessly to achieve your objective. You will need to
find ways around the obstacles you encounter. Through
persistence and determination you can succeed.

 If you sit back and allow your partner to dictate events, you
will feel miserable and unfulfilled. You need to set the pace.
You can achieve your goal in the long term, but you need to
be focused.

 This relationship is worth working on, but there are lots of
obstacles to overcome. It is well worth the effort. Visualize
your goal and do not waiver.

 There are problems in this friendship but they can be
resolved. They won't disappear overnight – be prepared to
confront and overcome each hurdle patiently.

 Don't be put off by a series of obstacles in your path. You
have the resources to overcome each problem one by one.
Stick to your inner conviction.

MOVING LINES

If you have just discovered a problem in your relationship, don't worry. You do have the resources to resolve this matter. Take immediate action to confront your partner over this issue and ensure action is taken straight away to address the situation.

Sometimes, tact is the missing ingredient in your approach to problem-solving. Try to think before you speak. Ultimately your sincerity will win through, but you could cause your partner unnecessary pain by your bluntness.

Now is a great time to address any problems in your relationship. You can quickly and easily resolve matters at this time. Think before you speak. This issue is not as serious as you first thought.

If you want to make lasting and mutually beneficial changes to your relationship, go ahead now. You have a perfect opportunity to increase your emotional fulfilment.

You are finding it easy to persuade your partner to go along with your way of thinking. You have won the battle but not the war. Keep the channels of communication open.

Do you really know what you want from this relationship? Don't push for what you might want. Pause and work out in your mind which circumstances would really satisfy you at this time.

○ EXISTING PARTNERSHIPS   ② NEW ROMANCE   ⑩ FRIENDSHIP   ⊗ PITFALLS

47 ISOLATION

Lake
Water

This is a period of time when what you say and do appears to have little effect on others. There is no point putting more effort into trying to win them over. Stay true to your heart.

If you feel like you're shouting at a brick wall, then you're right. This is an uncomfortable period when nothing you can say will alter matters. Bide your time.

There may be an attraction here, but there is very little communication. Do you want a relationship with someone who is not prepared to listen to your point of view?

If possible, take time out of this friendship. At present it is frustrating and unsupportive. The other person is unwilling to empathize with you.

Don't allow your spirits to be squashed by this feeling that you can't connect deeply to others. The time is simply not right. Take care of yourself and explore your creative side until conditions change.

MOVING LINES

Sadly, this relationship is not working out the way you would like. Although you can't alter the outcome, you can choose how you respond. Don't indulge in self-pity.

On the surface, this relationship appears to give you the emotional security and material support you need. The inner spark, however, is lacking. A new person or turn of events will shortly add passion to your life.

Your mind is confused and leading you astray. At present, you can't see your situation clearly and don't know who to trust. If this continues, you will be emotionally drained and sink into depression.

Go your own way. The advice friends and relatives are giving may be sincere but it will not help you overcome the problems you face. Follow your heart in this matter and make tough decisions.

You are in the right. You've followed your heart with honesty and integrity. Your true friends will support you through this difficult period. Stick to your principles.

You can free yourself from this relationship. Believe that you deserve and will gain more love and respect. Once you have made up your mind to make a change, you will feel much better.

---

① EXISTING PARTNERSHIPS   ② NEW ROMANCE   ⑩ FRIENDSHIP   ⊗ PITFALLS

48 COMMITMENT

Water
Wind

Commitment is the glue that holds relationships together. The issue here is a question of form. What sort of partnership do you want? Is marriage important to you? Do you need to agree on issues such as property, money or children?

Is it time to make your partnership official? This is an interesting period, when how you present yourself as a couple to the outside world is vitally important. Don't be afraid to formalize your commitment.

If you have just met someone, check that they are not committed elsewhere. Also make sure that there are no major obstacles from friends or family.

If you overstep the boundaries, you will find your friend's support drying up. It is vital you don't lean on anyone too much, or they may withdraw totally.

Danger: through enthusiasm, fear or neediness you'll draw too heavily on the other person's emotional strength. Try to maintain emotional equilibrium and don't pile your inadequacies on to your partner.

MOVING LINES

When a relationship is over, it is best simply to move on. There is no satisfaction in rehearsing the past in your mind. Let go or you will become depressed and frustrated.

There is the potential for a wonderful relationship, but one of you lacks the necessary commitment. Sadly, no progress can occur in such a situation. It is better to quit now rather than extend the period of pain.

You are ready and willing to have a monogamous relationship, but no partner is available at present. Stay true to your principles. The right person for you will appear in due course.

This is a time of preparation and inner work. You are clearing old blocks to your happiness. The outcome is good, in the longer term. For the present, count your blessings and be patient.

This relationship is slightly stuck at present. You both know what you want but haven't yet agreed how to achieve it. Act promptly or you will lose the emotional momentum.

Your partnership is a continual source of inspiration and emotional fulfilment. Any external obstacles only serve to strengthen your relationship. Take time to tell your partner how much you appreciate their love and support.

⓪ EXISTING PARTNERSHIPS   ② NEW ROMANCE   ⓪ FRIENDSHIP   ⊗ PITFALLS

49 RADICAL CHANGE

Lake
Flame

This is a time of abrupt, sweeping change. To create such a change and carry through the necessary measures takes vision, persistence and emotional strength. If you are not getting what you want from your partnership, seize this moment and go for your heart's desire.

 Has your partnership gone stale or have you lost sight of your original goal? Take time to reassess the situation carefully and then take radical action.

 No half measures are available here. Your life is about to be shaken from its foundations.

 This friendship is about to enter a new phase. However, you will have to push forcefully for any changes you seek.

 The danger here is that in your enthusiasm to create change you will be inconsiderate. Someone does have to lead the way and that someone is you – but be compassionate. Share your vision, communicate clearly and then act with dignity.

MOVING LINES

 You can see clearly what changes you would like to make. However, now is not the time to take the initiative. Be patient. Use the waiting time to be more creative and imaginative about potential solutions to your life issues.

 You have no alternative but to take drastic action. Prepare yourself carefully and make sure you have the support of friends and family. Do not be too proud to ask for emotional help, cash or a roof over your head if necessary.

 Timing is crucial here. You have felt uncomfortable about a situation for a while. First, try to reason with your partner. Second, try to gain help from a third party. Third, try to shock your partner with an ultimatum. If all this fails, make a radical break.

 If you have reasonable grounds for action, you'll gain the support of friends and family in making a break. The level of assistance you receive will be pleasantly surprising.

 You have already made up your mind and started to initiate the changes you seek. Trust your instinct. You are on the right path and your partner will accede to your requests in due course.

 Once you've achieved your objective, don't try to force the other person's hand further. Be content with your current progress. If you push your partner any more you may jeopardize what you have achieved.

◎ EXISTING PARTNERSHIPS   ⨂ NEW ROMANCE   ⑩ FRIENDSHIP   ⊗ PITFALLS

50 SPIRITUAL NOURISHMENT

Flame
Wind

Your relationship is strong and mutually supportive. It is built on love and respect. Whatever happens in the outside world, together you will be able to make the right decisions and take appropriate action. Do not be phased by short-term set-backs or obstacles, as these will only strengthen the bond you share together.

 You gain inspiration and understanding from your partner, and complement each other with your skills and talents. Together you can develop spiritually and prosper materially.

 Grab this person right away and don't let go. This is a marvellous chance to create a lasting partnership. Count your blessings.

 True friends are hard to find. Congratulations – you have discovered someone to share your life's journey. Enjoy discovering an easier way to relate to others.

 Be grateful for the chance to share your highest aspirations with a like-minded person. Share your good fortune, but don't boast about your happiness.

MOVING LINES

 You have the opportunity to turn this relationship into a more fulfilling one. However, first you need to let go of the emotional baggage from the past, as it's weighing you down.

 Focus on your partner and don't listen to gossip from outsiders. Keep true to yourself and try to avoid arguments about the nature of your relationship with friends and family.

 Your partner has not yet realized what a treasure you are. Your caring qualities and passionate nature will soon be recognized. This relationship will prosper in due course.

 You are playing fast and loose with the person you profess to love. No good will come of this. Shape up, take a good look at yourself and stop this self-deception. Only you know who you really love, but it is time you shared this knowledge with your partner.

 If you haven't already met a reliable partner, then you are about to meet the perfect match. Stay true to your dreams and don't opt for a quick fling. You will recognize the right person straight away and any short-term doubts you may have will evaporate quickly.

 This is a delightful partnership that works well on both the emotional and physical levels. You are also well suited spiritually and can communicate easily with each other.

51 UNEXPECTED NEWS

Thunder
Thunder

Y̶ou are in for a huge surprise. There is little point trying to work out in advance what's happening. Either your existing relationship is about to receive a jolt or, if you are single, prepare to be swept off your feet. How you respond to this change of fortune is up to you.

Your life together has been moving along in a humdrum way. Perhaps it is hard to imagine any other form of existence. Well, watch out – the universe has a big surprise for you!

If you have just met someone, this person is going to be a catalyst in your life. You will get the opportunity shortly to turn your life upside down. Only you can decide if you want to accept the challenge.

This friendship is about to be rocked by some extraordinary news. It will survive if you want it to.

The danger here is that you'll be so stunned by the news you will feel emotionally paralysed and unable to decide what your next move should be. Get counselling or outside help if necessary.

MOVING LINES

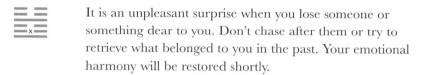

The news you receive will give you a jolt. You will be worried and concerned about how to cope. However, you will triumph and emerge emotionally stronger from the experience.

It is an unpleasant surprise when you lose someone or something dear to you. Don't chase after them or try to retrieve what belonged to you in the past. Your emotional harmony will be restored shortly.

Don't be paralysed by this surprise. Use your analytical mind to come up with a successful strategy so you can regain your emotional stability. Try to find the positive message hidden within the turmoil.

You feel as if you are emotionally cut off from people and the world. There is a numbness and unwillingness to accept what has happened. Seek support from family, friends or a good counsellor.

A series of small surprises changes the tempo of your emotional life to continually bumpy. Adjust to this new pattern and you will emerge stronger. If you try to regain control, you will become angry and frustrated.

The key to success at this time is inaction. Do not listen to friends and family (however well-meaning) who urge you to take a stand. Think things through carefully.

① EXISTING PARTNERSHIPS   ② NEW ROMANCE   ⑩ FRIENDSHIP   ⊗ PITFALLS

52 INNER PEACE

Mountain
Mountain

There is a time to act and a time to sow the seeds of future action in contemplation. Now is a time to go within, find your inner sanctuary of peace and visualize the future you desire. Use this opportunity to get rid of negative thought patterns and expand your vision of who you can become.

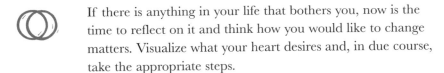

If there is anything in your life that bothers you, now is the time to reflect on it and think how you would like to change matters. Visualize what your heart desires and, in due course, take the appropriate steps.

If you have just met someone new, there has been a special heart-to-heart connection. You can revive each other's spirits simply by being together.

You must honour your need for time alone. If your friend can understand this and adjust to it, fine. If not, consider redefining the boundaries of your relationship.

Make sure you create enough time to be by yourself. Develop the powers of your mind. Do not let others talk you into hasty action on a matter of the heart.

MOVING LINES

 You are starting along a new path. Before you leap into this relationship or adopt a new pattern of behaviour, make sure you're following your heart. Check that you've healed the pain you've carried with you since childhood.

 When we are driven by inner demons, it is hard to stop. You may need counselling or help from friends to assist you in breaking this destructive pattern. Explore your creativity, play music or do some body work.

 The solution to your problem lies in meditation. It is also important to release tension from your body through exercise and expressing your creativity. Make sure you stick with a long-term programme of meditation.

 Your ego may have been bruised, but you have not lost anything essential. Count your blessings, meditate and visualize a more loving future. Try to widen your social circle and accept offers to explore new activities.

 Keep yourself to yourself. Avoid gossiping or pouring your heart out indiscriminately. If necessary, seek a professional counsellor to explore your feelings in safety and confidence.

 Congratulations! You are developing an ability to tune in to that inner source of peace, healing and inspiration. Remember that you have all the answers within. Try to meditate daily and keep in touch with nature. Go to the park, buy a bunch of flowers or plant some seeds.

⊙ EXISTING PARTNERSHIPS   ⊘ NEW ROMANCE   ⊚ FRIENDSHIP   ⊗ PITFALLS

53 SMOOTH PROGRESS

Wind
Mountain

This is a time when events and people will slot into place easily. It is as if your life has suddenly switched to a well-oiled track. Each step is the logical conclusion of the past one and the beginning of the next phase. Enjoy being in the flow.

Enjoy your partnership. Do not try to push to change the status quo abruptly. If you wish to persuade your partner of the value of a different approach to your relationship, you can succeed over time.

Don't rush into this relationship. The partnership is likely to take considerable time to develop, so be patient.

You can help each other by remaining supportive and calm. This is not a time for either of you to expect the other to devote more time to the friendship.

The danger here is twofold: either you will give up or try to push too hard. The watchwords are persistence and patience. You do have the formula for success.

MOVING LINES

 If you have just met someone and are unsure whether to ask them out, wait and see. You will see each other again in the normal course of events and can decide at a later date how you really feel.

 If you have just started going out with someone, you can enjoy this honeymoon period. Make sure you don't cut yourself off from your circle of friends.

 The position is hazardous. If you are tempted to push ahead with this relationship, it will backfire on you. Bide your time and then progress is possible. In the meantime, seek advice from close friends or family.

 You need to regain your composure and boost your self-esteem. Try to develop outside interests, meet like-minded people and, most of all, stop blaming yourself. You are doing your best.

 A rift has developed in your relationship and it will take time to heal. You can begin this healing process by opening your heart to the other person. This relationship can prosper.

 An ideal time to deepen and consecrate your relationship. Count your blessings and make sure your partner knows how much you care. Enjoy rekindling your passion.

ⓞ EXISTING PARTNERSHIPS   ⓞ NEW ROMANCE   ⓞ FRIENDSHIP   ⊗ PITFALLS

54 BRIEF ENCOUNTER

Thunder
Lake

It is important to be honest with yourself when you are involved with someone else. That way you have a chance to be honest with the other person about your real feelings. It is far better to admit to someone that you got involved in a moment of passion rather than lie to them and profess undying love.

 This partnership appears to lack a certain stability. Examine your goals and see whether your partner shares them. Face up to the reality of your relationship.

 Enjoy the passion and the attention, then move on. If you're meant to be together, doubtless it will happen in due course. Don't force the issue of commitment now.

 This friendship doesn't appear set to last in its current form. Do you really share the same interests and compatible viewpoints on life?

 The danger here is that you will clutch at emotional straws. Enjoy this relationship for what it is now, but do not try to build on it. Lust is not a reliable basis for a long-term partnership.

MOVING LINES

 This situation is complex. Your partner's affections are still tied up with another person. If you can live with this, fine. If not, reconsider your relationship. You deserve to have someone committed solely to you.

 Is your partner being faithful? Are they spending more time than you would like on friends and family? Through patience and persistence, you can make this relationship work.

 You appear willing to compromise your principles to win your share of love. Try boosting your self-esteem, and remember that you deserve a loving, committed partnership.

 You might think you have been left on the shelf. However, the ideal partner for you is about to appear in your life. Make sure you don't lock yourself away from people. Get out and about.

 There are some fundamental differences in beliefs and values between you and your partner. However, your love and good sense can survive these seemingly insurmountable problems.

 Neither party is being true to themselves. Both of you are holding back, perhaps through fear. The only way to succeed is for both of you to drop your defences and open your hearts.

55 FULFILMENT

Thunder
Flame

This is a very precious time, when your relationship can reach heights of passion and intimacy. Although unsustainable, this will provide incredible fulfilment, so enjoy this peak experience. Be grateful that you have reached this sense of oneness and don't blame yourself for its inevitable passing.

It's a great time to enjoy the fruits of all your hard work together. Celebrate your mutual achievements – get passionate, be spontaneous and enjoy being together.

What a wonderful, heady start to any relationship! You will be swept off your feet by your partner. Savour the moments and let yourself express your inner feelings.

A new sense of closeness will develop in this friendship. It will only last for a while, but will be the stuff of fond memories. Take advantage of this period of intimacy to deepen and strengthen your relationship.

Enjoy the moment. Don't analyze why this is happening – simply make the most of this opportunity for intimacy and passion.

MOVING LINES

 You needn't look outside this relationship for fresh experiences, as you can have these exciting and fulfilling dreams with your existing partner. Do whatever it takes to recapture the passion of your first few months together.

 Don't listen to gossips or jealous friends. Your partnership is special and unique. Enjoy it and plan a future together. Discuss how you can deepen your sense of commitment to each other.

 This relationship is going through a rocky patch. It's as if you've forgotten what brought you together in the first place. Try to remember what first attracted you to your partner. Take time to praise your mate's good qualities rather than focusing on the negative ones.

 A wonderful time is to be had. To make the most of it, spend a while focusing on how you'd like the future to develop. Then you can make concrete plans to achieve your goals together.

 You have a great deal of love and support around you. If you've been waiting for the right time to start a dream project, now is the moment. Go for it. Your partner, friends and family will surprise you with their inventiveness and practical support.

 If you push your partner now, you will get a nasty shock. This is not the right time to press for commitment. Back off or you could risk losing your mate.

Ⓞ EXISTING PARTNERSHIPS   ⦸ NEW ROMANCE   ⦿ FRIENDSHIP   ⊗ PITFALLS

56 FREE SPIRIT

Flame
Mountain

Sometimes it's best to explore life on your own. Relationships may seem an unnecessary weight to be carrying around. This is a period in your life when you want to be footloose and fancy free. Be careful you don't get drawn to the wrong people through a moment of lust or loneliness.

You may need to take time out from this relationship. Perhaps you should plan a holiday alone or start a new course. Explain carefully to your partner that your need is for more freedom, and that this doesn't mean you are looking for another person.

This relationship can be fun and frivolous. Don't expect commitment. Enjoy what is on offer and then move on.

You will need to explain to your friend that you need to be on your own, to travel and to meet new people.

This is probably just a phase, so don't dump existing partners and friends in your desire for free time. Be assertive and caring. Your true friends will understand your need for time alone, and they won't be clingy.

MOVING LINES

Don't get drawn into a series of meaningless flings. Stay true to yourself. You can enjoy this period of time without succumbing to mindless lust. If you have several affairs, you may deepen your feelings of being alone at this time.

You have the opportunity to create a relationship with someone rather different from your past choices. As long as you are sincere, you will have no regrets. Don't let friends or family interfere with your love life.

Don't play fast and loose with other people's affections, as you'll only create problems for yourself and those you claim to love. If you promise commitment and then change your mind, this person will try to seek revenge.

There is an inner tension and unhappiness. Outwardly all is well; you have the material success you crave. Remember – you deserve love as well. Try to restore some balance in your life and devote more time to your love life.

New relationships are possible now. You have the chance to explore aspects of your personality which in the past may have been hidden or ignored. Go for it.

This relationship is built on lust and impulse. It is not destined to last in its current form. Enjoy it while you can and then move on swiftly and gracefully.

57 SEEDS OF PASSION

Wind
Wind

If you have just met someone, then the new relationship has great possibilities. Each of you has the potential to change the other's perspective on life. This process will happen slowly and gradually. However, together you can develop this passion further.

 This is a time of gradual, almost inconspicuous change. You will look back on this period of time and realize a subtle shift for the better has taken place in your relationship.

 A slow-burning relationship. If you are content to be patient and open-minded, then this partnership could work for you.

 Over time you can reach an understanding – if not an agreement – on those issues currently creating conflict between you. Be patient.

 Don't be overambitious at this time. Powerful change can happen joyfully and easily without arguments or ultimatums. If you try too hard, you will simply run into an impasse.

MOVING LINES

So you don't know what to do? Try visualizing the likely outcome of alternative approaches. Then make a decision and stick to it. Don't ask friends or family for advice, as their views will only complicate the situation at this time.

You inner demons are playing havoc with your love life. Seek expert advice from a counsellor or healer on how to rid yourself of these emotional chains. Take the necessary time out of your busy schedule to address your emotional issues. It will be time well-spent.

Stop rehearsing events and conversations in your mind: make your decision and stick to it. If you keep prevaricating, you will lose respect and feel powerless. Seize the moment and go for your heart's desire.

You know the time is right to go for what you want, and have all the emotional resources needed to succeed. If you act ruthlessly, swiftly and decisively now, you can win your heart's desire.

Improve this relationship through negotiating a new set of conditions with your partner, but do this calmly and confidently. Change will not happen overnight, so monitor the situation carefully.

You know what is wrong, but now is not the time to improve matters. Spend time with like-minded people, take care of your health and delay taking any action on this matter.

① EXISTING PARTNERSHIPS ② NEW ROMANCE ③ FRIENDSHIP ⊗ PITFALLS

58 MUTUAL HAPPINESS

Lake
Lake

This is an enjoyable period in your life, when you can create new patterns of happiness. We often learn from our parents what makes us happy; now is a time to discover joy in the small things of life. Count your blessings each night before you go to sleep, and focus on all the good in your life.

Have fun together, as your love can be a source of mutual happiness. Nurture each other. If one of you is a little depressed, the other can easily lift your spirits.

Enjoy this honeymoon period. Have fun, rediscover the joy of childhood and be spontaneous. Explore new places or activities together.

This friendship is full of laughter and mutual support. True friends are hard to find and now you have the opportunity to enjoy a mutually caring relationship.

Be open to new experiences and people. You won't gain the full benefit of this period if you close yourself off through fear. Now you can drop some of the defences you've carefully constructed throughout your life.

MOVING LINES

 You don't need to rush around or party – your happiness comes from sharing quiet, intimate moments with your partner. Have fun, and be inventive and passionate.

 You're tempted to have a fling with someone who is unreliable. Don't let lust get the better of you. Stay away from this person and you'll have no regrets. If you succumb to temptation, the consequences will be traumatic.

 If you're trying to bury your feelings in a series of one-night stands, it won't help: your self-esteem will simply get a further knock. Consider counselling or a self-assertiveness course.

 You're being tempted to have a fling. True, it would put some passion into your life but the cost would be high. Seek other forms of amusement. Learn a new skill, play sport or develop your creativity.

 Someone or something poses a threat to your emotional wellbeing. Don't develop a craving for a particular person, or let an addiction to any substance, ruin your peace of mind. Distinguish clearly between love and lust.

 You're about to be seduced by someone who doesn't have your interests at heart. Is the short-term pleasure of passion really worth the long-term pain of regret? Look within and focus clearly on your goals.

◑ EXISTING PARTNERSHIPS   ⊘ NEW ROMANCE   ◐ FRIENDSHIP   ⊗ PITFALLS

59 RELEASING EMOTIONAL BARRIERS

Wind
Water

Before you can enjoy an intimate and fulfilling relationship with another, you need to let go of the emotional walls you've built as protection. You have a safe opportunity within this relationship to dissolve your defensive barriers gradually. Take this chance and open your heart.

You can reach a new level of intimacy now. Childhood fears can be dissolved and old patterns of defence released. You can enjoy a new sense of emotional flow.

Use this opportunity to heal your broken heart and release any negative images of yourself. Love can heal the past in a very powerful and profound way.

This is a great chance to develop a true friendship and let go of old traumas. Boost each other's self-esteem, be spontaneous and have a bit of fun.

Don't cling to past patterns out of fear. If necessary, seek the help of a counsellor – someone to assist you in your healing process.

MOVING LINES

 If you don't address your own emotional makeup, you will create problems in this relationship. Try self-help tapes, a personal-development workshop or counselling.

 There is a great deal of emotional support around you. Open your heart to receive this love and nurturing. This is a time of profound potential healing so long as you are prepared to accept the assistance which is on offer now.

 You have become so attached to a material goal that it's blocking your relationship. Stop trying so hard to achieve what you think will make you happy. Enjoy the love this relationship has to offer.

 Sometimes we need to release old relationships and move on. Now is such a time: be bold and take a step into the unknown. Open your heart and make room for a new person.

 You have reached an emotional crisis. Congratulations! This can be a turning point in your life. Go for true love and don't allow anyone to treat you as a second-class citizen.

 This relationship is mutually destructive. You have the insight and strength to prevent further emotional damage. Take steps to end this painful experience as soon as it is practical to do so. Seek legal help if necessary.

◐ EXISTING PARTNERSHIPS   ② NEW ROMANCE   ⓝ FRIENDSHIP   ⊗ PITFALLS

60 DEFINE YOUR LIMITS

Water
Lake

The issue here is what is acceptable behaviour in this relationship. Is monogamy important? Do you share your money? Is your home owned equally by both parties? And who looks after any children? In order to enjoy a partnership truly, you need to agree (and then follow) some clear guidelines.

Is your partner pulling their weight? Are you providing the financial support as well as the emotional? Reassess your relationship and, if necessary, be firm in your demand for more help from your partner.

Watch out – this person may take more from you than you expect. Are you playing the role of rescuer? Don't start by giving more support than you receive; otherwise, you will feel drained.

Make sure you don't get sucked into your friend's emotional problems. If you're involved with someone who is continually demanding attention, be firm and less available for them.

Everyone loves to be needed. However, relationships with very demanding people are draining and ultimately unfulfilling. Steer clear of users and emotional vampires.

MOVING LINES

 If you stick to the agreement you've negotiated with your partner, you will benefit from the greater security and love created by this relationship. This will give you the necessary confidence to achieve your goals.

 You have an opportunity to explore a new relationship. Be honest with your existing partner, explain any problems you see in your relationship and then, if necessary, make your move.

 Don't try to protect the one you love from their responsibilities. If you allow your partner to behave in a selfish or childish way, the relationship will struggle.

 Once you have agreed a set of mutually acceptable guidelines, this relationship will flourish. You will have more enthusiasm for projects and more energy to channel into common goals.

 Are you asking more of your partner than you're willing to give? Try to reverse the roles and show good faith by proving your loyalty and trust in a tangible way. Success is assured.

 Don't give into temptation. You will cause yourself a great deal of emotional pain if you have a quick fling or empty the joint account to finance an impulsive spending spree.

◎ EXISTING PARTNERSHIPS   ② NEW ROMANCE   ⑩ FRIENDSHIP   ⊗ PITFALLS

61 UNDERSTANDING

Wind
Lake

This issue is complex. Two people are looking at a situation from conflicting standpoints. To resolve this problem you need to be able to understand the other's point of view, then explain how your goal can help them as well. Communication is the key.

Just because you view the world differently doesn't mean you can't reach an agreement. It just means you'll have to put more effort into convincing the other person. Patience and persistence will prevail.

This relationship will be tough to start with. Although you are strongly attracted to this person you need to consider carefully if your differences can be overcome.

On the surface it is hard to see what's keeping this friendship together. Do you enjoy conflict and argument? Take a cool look at this relationship and decide on some mutual goals.

There is quite a deep-seated problem here, but it can be overcome with sufficient patience and commitment. Don't start something you aren't prepared to continue.

MOVING LINES

Don't involve a third party in your relationship problems. Tempting as it may be to seek outside support, it will backfire and create jealousy and tension. You need a cool head and a warm heart to resolve this issue.

Something has been worrying you, but you and your partner can reach an understanding over this. Stay true to your feelings and express yourself clearly and calmly. A resolution will come more quickly and easily than you imagined.

You've allowed your happiness to be completely tied up with this other person. This means you've lost control of your emotional wellbeing. Try to regain your emotional integrity.

If you are weighing up two options, choose the path of your heart. Other people's rationalizations or preferences are not reliable guides. If necessary, spend some time alone in order to discover your true feelings.

You are calm and confident. You can win your partner over to your point of view. Allow them time to adjust their position and don't be tempted to use emotional blackmail as a weapon in this battle of wills.

What is being said is at cross-purposes with what is being done. Analyze your behaviour and that of your partner. Remember: there's more to love than saying the three words 'I love you'.

ⓞ EXISTING PARTNERSHIPS   ② NEW ROMANCE   ⑩ FRIENDSHIP   ⊗ PITFALLS

A LOW PROFILE

Thunder
Mountain

This is a time for maintaining the status quo through patience and calmness. If rows over family matters occur, try to see things from a broader perspective and open your heart to your partner's friends and family. Don't get drawn into arguments at this time.

 It may be a bit boring having to spend more time with your partner's family, friends or boss, but this is a time to show your solidarity.

 Are you going out with this person because you are attracted to them, or out of a sense of obligation? Examine your motives carefully before you get involved further.

 This friendship has become stultified. You seem to feel it's your duty to help this other person. Don't let resentment and frustration build up.

 Don't issue ultimatums or expect speedy progress here. Emotionally, life is rather grey at present. Treat yourself to some fun times with like-minded people and explore new activities.

MOVING LINES

 If you're thinking about an outrageous solution to this issue, don't be tempted. Sadly, there is no quick fix. Talk things through calmly and don't expect any easy solutions to appear.

 Do not run away from your problems – the answer lies in better communication. Give your partner a chance to change. Try not to blame the other person for how you feel.

 You might hold the high moral ground but in this case that doesn't automatically mean you'll succeed. Your partner is about to spring a surprise on you. Try to be flexible in your response and don't say anything that will limit your options.

 Keep visualizing your goal. Be patient, firm and keep out of arguments. Persistence and inner confidence will help you triumph here. It is not the right time for action at the moment.

 You need help from outside this relationship to identify and address this problem. Seek the assistance of a counsellor, friends or family. If necessary, get some legal advice.

 If you push for greater commitment now, you'll trigger a breakup instead. Stay calm, and be loving to your partner. Your love will help melt their fear of greater intimacy.

Ⓒ EXISTING PARTNERSHIPS   Ⓡ NEW ROMANCE   Ⓕ FRIENDSHIP   ⊗ PITFALLS

63 SEEDS OF CONFLICT

Water
Flame

On the surface everything appears fine, but the seeds of conflict have been sown. Take this opportunity to continue to discuss your goals and dreams. Enjoy the status quo, but don't sweep any problems under the carpet. More communication is the answer.

 Having gone through a difficult patch, your relationship is improving. By all means celebrate, but don't ignore small differences. Try to discuss your feelings more openly with your partner.

 After a difficult spell in your life, you feel happy and relieved to have met this person. Don't let your new-found enthusiasm override your reason.

 Your friendship has been strengthened by past events and is back on an even keel. However, certain issues still remain unresolved. Sort them out sooner rather than later.

 Don't allow small conflicts to be overlooked. That's a recipe for frustration and fuel for future arguments. Talk matters over as quickly as possible.

MOVING LINES

 Your partnership is not solid enough yet to withstand much external pressure. Spend some more time together building up mutual trust and understanding. Try to listen to what your partner is actually saying rather than what you hope they're saying.

 You may feel neglected or misunderstood, and issuing an ultimatum will not help matters. Time will heal this problem. In the meantime, friends and family can provide support and material assistance.

 You have reached a new level of intimacy with your partner. Enjoy it, and don't push for further commitment as this would cause unnecessary tension. Celebrate your relationship and count your blessings.

 In reaching this reconciliation you may have chosen to overlook some weakness in your partner. If this weak point is not addressed and remedied, more problems will occur shortly.

 Don't be won over by flattery or grand gestures of love. Remember – it's how your partner treats you on a daily basis that's important. Practise tough love. If necessary, issue that ultimatum and stick to it.

 Forgive and forget, but don't pretend to forgive and then keep reminding your partner of their old faults. You can move forward now to a more fulfilling relationship, so long as you are prepared to leave the past behind you.

Ⓞ EXISTING PARTNERSHIPS   ② NEW ROMANCE   Ⓝ FRIENDSHIP   ⊗ PITFALLS

64 METAMORPHOSIS

Flame
Water

Times of change tend to be difficult. If you are sincere and take things easy, you can create a fulfilling new relationship now. Trying to speed up the process will not achieve anything. Like fine wines, relationships can get better as they mature.

 You are on the verge of making a commitment to this person. Take your time. There are plenty of issues to resolve and practical matters to arrange, so enjoy this time of anticipation.

 You may have already decided that this is the one for you, but the other person needs time to reach the same conclusion. Take it slowly.

 Friendship is about to blossom and events are moving the pair of you closer together. You'll shortly be able to enjoy a greater intimacy.

 If you rush headlong into a commitment, you'll miss a vital part of this particular emotional jigsaw puzzle. Fulfilment is within your reach. Be patient and you will get your heart's desire.

MOVING LINES

 Now is not the right time to achieve your goal. If you push blindly ahead you will meet with failure, so bide your time. There is a third party blocking your way.

 This is the moment to sow the seeds of your future success. It is too early to make a move, but you can fine-tune your plan and gather moral support from friends and family.

 The time to act is now, but you do need help from your friends or family, or perhaps a counsellor. Don't be too proud to ask for assistance. Pay attention to practical matters such as money and a roof over your head.

 You can achieve your goal now, but you'll need to be single-minded and persistent. Keep yourself positive and do what you can to boost your self-esteem. It may help to take a course or study a self-development book.

 Congratulations! Enjoy the fruits of your success. There is a new vibrancy and passion in your relationship as well as greater compassion and tenderness. You can build a long-term partnership on this stable foundation.

 Celebrate by all means, but don't be tempted to overstep the mark. This relationship is at a tender stage and you don't want to jeopardize your hard-won trust. There are still many vital and controversial issues that need to be resolved.

◐ EXISTING PARTNERSHIPS   ⦸ NEW ROMANCE   ⦿ FRIENDSHIP   ⊗ PITFALLS

RECORD SHEET

RELATIONSHIP:

QUESTION	DATE:TIME PLACE	HEXAGRAMS I	HEXAGRAMS II	INSIGHTS	OUTCOME

FURTHER READING

Chia, Mantak, *Transform Stress into Vitality*. New York: Healing Tao Books Inc., 1985.

Cleary, Thomas, *The Secret of the Golden Flower*. San Francisco: Harper San Francisco, 1991.

Eberhard, Wolfram, *Dictionary of Chinese Symbols*. London: Routledge & Kegan Paul, 1986.

Metz, Pamela K. and Jacqueline L. Tobin, *The Tao of Women*. Shaftesbury: Element, 1996.

Mitchell, Stephen (trans.), *Tao Te Ching: The Book of the Way*, Lao-Tzu. London: Kyle Cathie, 1996.

Reid, Daniel, *The Tao of Health, Sex and Longevity*. London: Simon and Schuster, 1989.

Rossbach, Sarah and Lin Yun, *Living Colour*. New York: Kodansha International, 1994.

Wilhelm, Richard (trans.), *The I Ching or Book of Changes*. London: Routledge & Kegan Paul, 1951 (first edition).

Yü, Lu K'uan, *Taoist Yoga*. London: Rider, 1970.

ACKNOWLEDGEMENTS

AUTHOR'S ACKNOWLEDGEMENTS

To my clients whose questions inspired this book, to Julie Carpenter and Aziz Khan for their illustrations, to Elaine Partington for her visual perspicacity, to Tessa Monina for project management, to Ian Jackson for his enthusiasm and support, and to Lisa Dyer for masterminding this second edition.

TABLE OF HEXAGRAMS

1 (page 14)	2 (page 16)	3 (page 18)	4 (page 20)	5 (page 22)	6 (page 24)	7 (page 26)	8 (page 28)
9 (page 30)	10 (page 32)	11 (page 34)	12 (page 36)	13 (page 38)	14 (page 40)	15 (page 42)	16 (page 44)
17 (page 46)	18 (page 48)	19 (page 50)	20 (page 52)	21 (page 54)	22 (page 56)	23 (page 58)	24 (page 60)
25 (page 62)	26 (page 64)	27 (page 66)	28 (page 68)	29 (page 70)	30 (page 72)	31 (page 74)	32 (page 76)
33 (page 78)	34 (page 80)	35 (page 82)	36 (page 84)	37 (page 86)	38 (page 88)	39 (page 90)	40 (page 92)
41 (page 94)	42 (page 96)	43 (page 98)	44 (page 100)	45 (page 102)	46 (page 104)	47 (page 106)	48 (page 108)
49 (page 110)	50 (page 112)	51 (page 114)	52 (page 116)	53 (page 118)	54 (page 120)	55 (page 122)	56 (page 124)
57 (page 126)	58 (page 128)	59 (page 130)	60 (page 132)	61 (page 134)	62 (page 136)	63 (page 138)	64 (page 140)